prépabac

COURS & ENTRAÎNEMENT

1re toutes séries

Anglais

LV1 - LV2

- **Catherine Terré**
  Professeur au lycée Lakanal (Sceaux)
- **Pierre Péhaut**
  Professeur au lycée Pierre-de-Fermat (Toulouse)
- **Sophie Béthery-Dostes**
  Agrégée de l'Université
  Professeur au lycée Lakanal (Sceaux)

Hatier

Conception graphique : Frédéric Jély
Mise en page : Michelle Bourgeois
Iconographie : Hatier Illustration
Cartographie : Corédoc

978-2-218-99467-8

Mode d'emploi

Votre ouvrage Prépabac

Conforme au dernier programme de langues vivantes du cycle terminal et aux nouvelles épreuves du baccalauréat, ce « Prépabac » vous propose un **outil de travail** très complet.

Vous y trouverez :

- des **cours** détaillés ;
- des fiches de **méthode** en vue du bac ;
- des révisions **grammaticales** ;
- des **exercices** progressifs pour vous entraîner **à l'écrit et à l'oral**, suivis d'un **sujet** de type bac et de leurs **corrigés** détaillés.

COURS | MÉTHODE | EXERCICES | CORRIGÉS

Enrichies de nombreux **commentaires** et **conseils**, toutes ces ressources vous permettent d'aborder en confiance vos contrôles durant l'année et de vous préparer **dès la 1re** à l'épreuve du bac.

Vos ressources en ligne

Tous les **documents audio** associés à cet ouvrage sont accessibles gratuitement sur **www.prepabac.com/media** par la saisie de mots clés figurant dans l'ouvrage. Ils sont signalés par le pictogramme .

sommaire

LES MÉTHODES DU BAC

Compréhension de l'écrit

Expression écrite

Compréhension de l'oral

Expression orale

GRAMMAIRE : 12 POINTS CLÉS

Les méthodes du bac

CHAPITRE

1 Lire et comprendre un document

Quand vous lisez un texte en anglais, vous commencez par en comprendre les idées principales. C'est précisément sur la compréhension générale des textes que portent les premières questions de compréhension de l'écrit au baccalauréat. Cet exercice porte sur deux textes qui peuvent être illustrés par un document iconographique. Vous trouverez ci-dessous des conseils pour bien répondre.

I Lire la « carte d'identité » du texte

- Les textes peuvent être des extraits d'œuvre de fiction ou d'article de presse. Dans les deux cas, il est nécessaire de prendre connaissance du **titre** ainsi que des **références** et de la **source** qui figurent sous les textes.
- Pour un **extrait de fiction**, la date de parution doit être interprétée avec prudence : un roman publié en 2008 peut raconter une histoire qui se passe en 1940 ou même au Moyen Âge ! Si l'extrait a un **titre** particulier, différent de celui de l'œuvre dont il est tiré, regardez-le de très près : il a été conçu pour vous mettre sur la piste des éléments fondamentaux de l'extrait.
- Dans le cas d'un **article de presse**, la source vous renseignera sur le **type de périodique** (journal ou magazine) et sur l'**origine géographique** (anglaise, américaine...) de celui-ci.
- Le texte peut aussi être précédé d'une **introduction**. Lisez-la attentivement : elle contient des renseignements indispensables à la compréhension de l'extrait.

II Lire « utile »

A Première lecture

Lisez le texte intégralement et concentrez-vous sur ce que vous comprenez. Pas de défaitisme, pas de panique : pensez à vous aider des mots transparents et déduisez toujours le sens des mots en respectant le **contexte**.

B Seconde lecture

Si le texte est accompagné d'un questionnaire complet (compréhension générale et approfondie), vous pouvez, à ce stade, prendre connaissance des premières questions, celles qui correspondent en principe à la compréhension générale. Relisez ensuite le texte, toujours dans son intégralité. Vous pouvez surligner ce que vous comprenez lors de cette seconde lecture.

III Faire un bilan de la compréhension globale

A Article de presse

Il faut être capable de rendre compte des contextes géographique et historique de l'article, ainsi que du sujet traité et des personnes impliquées. Quand le texte s'y prête, il faudra aussi comprendre les enjeux de la question abordée par le journaliste.

B Extrait de fiction

Assurez-vous que vous êtes capable de bien répondre aux questions de compréhension générale : ***who? where? when? what (happens)?*** Et, éventuellement : ***why?*** et ***how?***

- ***Who?*** Il s'agit d'identifier **les personnages** et **le narrateur**.

• Rappelez-vous que, dans un texte, un même personnage peut être désigné de plusieurs façons : avec des pronoms, bien sûr, mais aussi des prénoms, des diminutifs, des surnoms. Par exemple, un personnage qui apparaît d'abord sous le nom de *Robert Hawks* pourra devenir *Bob* quelques lignes plus bas, puis être désigné à l'aide de l'expression *the fat man*. Un autre personnage, *Amanda*, deviendra *the tall blonde*, ou encore *Mandy*, pour se transformer en *Mrs O'Brien*.

• Identifiez leur **sexe**. Aidez-vous des pronoms personnels et des déterminants possessifs ; ceux-ci sont très informatifs en anglais. Par exemple : *Sam was furious. Her car had broken down again. Her* nous apprend que *Sam* est une femme *(Samantha)*. Si cela est possible, repérez l'**âge** des personnages. Identifiez les **liens** qui les unissent : se connaissent-ils ? S'agit-il de parents, d'amis, de collègues ?

• Une fois que vous avez répondu à ces questions, vous pouvez vous demander si l'on entrevoit les qualités ou les défauts des personnages, leurs sentiments, leurs intentions.

■ *Where?* Il s'agit de repérer **le lieu** où se passe la scène. Les faits relatés dans le passage peuvent se dérouler en plusieurs endroits. Regardez de près tous les noms communs et tous les noms propres qui peuvent renvoyer à un lieu : *town, city, park, swimming-pool, Aberdeen, Scotland*, etc. Cependant, il se peut qu'un texte ne fournisse aucune indication sur le lieu où se passe la scène.

■ *When?* Il s'agit de repérer **l'époque, le moment** où se passent la scène et les différentes **étapes** de l'action.

• Le récit contenu dans un extrait, même si celui-ci est court, peut couvrir plusieurs jours, voire plusieurs années. L'auteur peut faire des allers et retours entre le passé et le présent. Il peut tout à coup regarder vers l'avenir. Autant dire que, pour bien répondre à la question *when?*, vous devez être très attentif aux temps et aux formes des verbes.

• La plupart des textes sont écrits au prétérit *(worked)* : dans ce contexte, un *past perfect (had worked)* indique un retour en arrière, vers un passé plus lointain (→ p. 185).

As they **had met** before, she expected him to remember her.
Comme ils s'étaient déjà rencontrés, elle s'attendait à ce qu'il se souvienne d'elle.

• Rappelez-vous que le *present perfect* simple *(have worked)* ou en *-ing (has been working)* n'est pas un temps du passé : il est toujours, d'une façon ou d'une autre, intimement lié au moment présent (→ p. 185 et 186).

She **has been** ill for a week.
Cela **fait** une semaine qu'elle est malade.

• Des événements passés peuvent également être relatés au présent, même si c'est plus rare.

• Cependant, il peut arriver qu'un texte ne fournisse aucune indication sur le moment où se passe la scène.

• Repérez les indicateurs de temps, de chronologie ou de fréquence. Voici les plus fréquents.

ZOOM

Les indicateurs de temps (chronologie et fréquence)

mots / expressions	exemples
first (of all), firstly : premièrement, tout d'abord	First, let's read the introduction.
then, next, after that, afterwards, subsequently : puis, ensuite	Subsequently, we'll read the text.
soon : bientôt, peu de temps après	She soon realised that Gerald was not a gentleman.
finally, eventually, in the end : finalement, au bout du compte at the end of : à la fin de	She refused to have any contact with him, but eventually agreed to read his letters.
meanwhile, in the meantime : entre temps, sur ces entrefaites	Leave the kitchen floor to dry. Meanwhile, make the beds.
as : alors que, au moment où, au fur et à mesure que	As he grew older, he realised that Jessie had been right about their mother.
while : pendant que	Why don't you walk the dog while I shower?
as soon as : dès que	Joshua called me as soon as he found my passport.
on + V-ing, upon + V-ing : au moment (même) où	On hearing the news, Alex smiled for the first time in months.
hardly, no sooner : à peine	Hardly had he shut the door when he realised he had left his keys inside. No sooner had Bob arrived than he started shouting at us.
hardly ever : presque jamais, rarement	Miss Walters hardly ever spoke to her neighbours.
rarely, seldom : rarement	Mr Piper seldom leaves his armchair.
(every) now and then, (every) now and again, from time to time, occasionally : de temps à autre	Every now and again, she opened the window to air the room.

■ ***What happens?*** Il s'agit de repérer les **principaux événements**.

> **ATTENTION !**
> Tous les événements n'ont pas nécessairement la même importance.

• On peut vous demander de travailler sur la nature et la chronologie des événements. On peut aussi vous faire reconstituer leur enchaînement logique, leurs causes, leurs manifestations.

• Si vous avez le sentiment qu'il ne se passe pas grand-chose, demandez-vous, par exemple, ce que l'extrait vous apprend sur le(s) personnage(s), sur un événement qui a déjà eu lieu, ou qui va se produire.

■ ***Why? How?*** Il s'agit de comprendre les causes et les manifestations des événements.

• Les **causes** peuvent être repérées à l'aide de mots tels que *because, because of, as, since* (puisque), *considering that, due to, owing to, thanks to* (grâce à)...

• La **façon dont se manifestent** les événements peut être suggérée par des adverbes (→ p. 166-169), des structures du type *He shot him dead* (Il le tua d'un coup de feu), *She kicked the door shut* (Elle ferma la porte d'un coup de pied).

• Notez que, pour exprimer le pourquoi et le comment des événements, l'auteur utilise souvent des procédés subtils. Nous entrons alors dans le domaine de la compréhension approfondie et de l'implicite.

IV Comprendre mieux : la compréhension approfondie

■ Les principes et les conseils que nous vous avons donnés ci-dessus restent valables pour répondre aux questions de compréhension approfondie. Nous y ajouterons les suivants.

■ Avant de vous atteler à la compréhension approfondie, **relisez les questions** auxquelles vous devez répondre. Puis, observez le texte de très près. Vous pouvez utiliser des crayons de couleurs pour créer un « code couleurs » : par exemple si vous décidez que la question 5 sera la question bleue, vous soulignez en bleu les mots, les parties du texte qui contiennent des éléments de réponse à cette question. Bien sûr, un même mot, un même passage peuvent avoir plusieurs rôles, surtout dans un texte littéraire. Il se peut, par conséquent, que certains éléments portent plusieurs couleurs.

ZOOM

Lexique de la compréhension de texte

a character, the main character, a minor character: un personnage (principal ≠ secondaire)

Relations between Ann and Paul are strained (tendues).

a conflict, a disagreement between A and B

An unexpected event occurs. Un événement inattendu se produit.

a twist: un rebondissement

embody, the embodiment of: incarner, l'incarnation de

symbolize, a symbol, symbolic of

raise an issue: soulever un problème

show someone's true motives: révéler les motivations réelles de qqn

The author / The journalist explains / analyses / criticises.

imply: suggérer

a clue: un indice

depict, a depiction of

Ann is depicted (décrite, dépeinte) as a calculating woman.

explain (something to someone), an explanation of

The word "shame" occurs three times (apparaît trois fois).

The tone is serious / sad / depressing / funny / light.

the gist /dʒɪst/ of the passage: l'essentiel du passage

The author's / The journalist's purpose was to show / must have been to show / may have been to show that... Le but de l'auteur / du journaliste était de montrer / était sûrement de montrer / était probablement de montrer que...

RÉCAPITULONS

- La compréhension d'un texte s'effectue en plusieurs étapes quelle que soit la nature du texte.
- Il faut d'abord tenir compte de la source, lire le texte au moins deux fois en répondant aux questions de compréhension globale et enfin se concentrer sur l'implicite.

Comprendre un article de presse

LA DÉMARCHE

- Je dois tenir compte des éléments autour du texte.
- Je lis le texte en pensant aux questions de compréhension globale.
- Je relis le texte en prenant garde à l'implicite.

L'EXEMPLE COMMENTÉ

Revolutionary Words

"Most great book lists concentrate on works of the highest literary or scholarly merit. Happily, the Library of Congress's exhibition, "The Books That Shaped America", ignores the familiar high-culture shibboleths and embraces cookbooks (Irma Rombauer's *The Joy of Cooking*) and schoolbooks (McGuffey's *Primer*), mysteries (Dashiell Hammett's *Red Harvest*) and science fiction (Ray Bradbury's *Fahrenheit 451*), political tracts as well as poetry, both Dr Seuss and Dr Spock.

When first published, these books shocked people, made them angry, shook up their deepest beliefs. They shamed readers with accounts of racism, greed, corruption, Puritanism and provincial narrow-mindedness. [...] Just skimming through the titles of "The Books That Shaped America" underscores that in the US anything can be questioned, everything can be changed.

If, however, there is any single, great American theme, it is self-transformation. So here are Benjamin Franklin's autobiography, that stirring guidebook to personal improvement, and Frederick Douglass's account of his years of slavery and his escape from it. Here, too, is one of Horatio Alger Jr.'s rags-to-riches novels, and Edgar Rice Burroughs's great bildungsroman *Tarzan of the Apes*, and Fitzgerald's *The Great Gatsby*, and even Dale Carnegie's *How to Win Friends and Influence People*. Jefferson spoke of "life, liberty and the pursuit of happiness", but he might just as well have said: Become who you truly are.

The *Washington Post* in the *Guardian Weekly*, July 13, 2012.

shibboleth: « vache sacrée »
bildungsroman: roman d'apprentissage
L'expression "life, liberty and the pursuit of happiness" est tirée de la Déclaration d'Indépendance des États Unis (4 juillet 1776).

POUR VOUS AIDER

The Guardian Weekly est une édition anglaise hebdomadaire rassemblant les principaux articles du *Guardian*, de *the Observer*, du *Monde* et du *Washington Post*. Ici, c'est l'origine américaine de l'article qui prime.

- Le paragraphe qui suit montre les différentes étapes de la compréhension.
- Les éléments « autour du texte » sont signalés en **noir**. Le contexte est indiqué en **vert**. Le sujet général en **bleu** et les éléments de la compréhension approfondie en **rose**.

The article was primarily published in an American newspaper. So the context is likely to be American as well.
The title, "Revolutionary Words", is an allusion to the Revolutionary War which is the name given to the American War of Independence, but the term "words" announces the topic of literature developed in the text.
The introduction contains the main information: the famous Library of Congress in Washington, D.C. has recently published a reading list encapsulating the American spirit of independence.
The journalist's purpose is to show that the books in the reading list entitled "The Books That Shaped America" have been aptly selected since they convey a major American characteristic, namely, self-improvement and fulfilment, along with the notion that nothing should be taken for granted. In order to prove his point, he gives some examples which indeed show that even though there is a wide range of books, they all remind the reader of the same idea.

to encapsulate: incarner
to convey: traduire, évoquer

SE TESTER QUIZ

1 Repérer les référents des pronoms personnels et des adjectifs possessifs ainsi que les appellations des personnages

Lisez le texte et cochez la réponse qui convient.

“ [The] fact was that **his father had died** a full month before **Thérèse** walked out on him, and if he had had some inkling of the money he was about to inherit, he probably could have talked her into staying. Even if she hadn't stayed, there would have been no need to **take Juliette out to Minnesota to live with his sister** [...]. But he still had his job with the fire department back then, and how was he supposed to take care of a two-year-old child when his work kept him out of the house at all hours of the day and night? If there had been some money, he would have hired a woman to live with them and look after Juliette. [...] It wasn't that his salary was so bad, but **his mother's stroke four years ago** had emptied him out, and he was still spending monthly payments down to the rest home in Florida where she had died. Given all that, his sister's place had seemed like the only solution. At least Juliette would have a chance to live with a real family, to be surrounded by other kids and to breathe some fresh air, and that was a lot better than anything he could offer her himself. Then, out of the blue, **the lawyer found him** and **the money fell into his lap**.

Paul Auster, *The Music of Chance*, 1990.

walked out on him: l'avait quitté	monthly payments: remboursements mensuels
inkling: la moindre idée	out of the blue: sans qu'il s'y attende
talk sb into: convaincre qqn de	the money fell into his lap: il s'est retrouvé avec plein d'argent
stroke: attaque (AVC)	
emptied out: ruiné	

1. “his” (l. 1) renvoie à :
- ☐ **a.** the main character's father
- ☐ **b.** Thérèse's father
- ☐ **c.** the main character's

2. “he” (l. 2) renvoie à :
- ☐ **a.** the main character's father
- ☐ **b.** Thérèse's father
- ☐ **c.** the main character

3. "she" (l. 3) renvoie à :
- ☐ **a.** Juliette
- ☐ **b.** Thérèse
- ☐ **c.** the main character's sister

4. "a two-year-old child" (l. 6) fait référence à :
- ☐ **a.** Juliette
- ☐ **b.** Thérèse
- ☐ **c.** the main character's sister

5. "them" (l. 8) renvoie à :
- ☐ **a.** the main character and a woman
- ☐ **b.** the main character and Juliette
- ☐ **c.** the main character and Thérèse

6. "she" (l. 11) renvoie à :
- ☐ **a.** Juliette
- ☐ **b.** Thérèse
- ☐ **c.** the main character's mother

7. "that" (l. 14) renvoie à :
- ☐ **a.** breathe some fresh air
- ☐ **b.** live with a real family, be surrounded by other kids and breathe some fresh air
- ☐ **c.** fresh air

8. "his" (l. 15) renvoie à :
- ☐ **a.** the lawyer's
- ☐ **b.** the main character's
- ☐ **c.** the money

S'ENTRAÎNER

2 Repérer la chronologie des événements

Relisez le texte de l'exercice 1 et classez les événements en gras dans l'ordre chronologique, de 1 à 6.

OBJECTIF BAC

3 Répondre aux questions de compréhension

Lisez le texte intégralement. Puis relisez-le et répondez aux questions de base *(who, where, when, what happens, consequences)*.

"Britain may have been in the grip of recession, but it seemed to have had little impact on those select members of the aristocracy and business community who attended the ceremony and afterwards convened at the country seat of the Carfax family for a lavish party which was still going strong (according to at least one of the newspaper reports) at four o'clock the next afternoon.

The party, in fact, lasted longer than the marriage.

Mark and Lady Frances had departed the revels early in the evening and joined a flight to Nice: from there, a taxi took them to Mark's villa on the Riviera, where they were to begin their honeymoon. They arrived shortly after midnight, and slept in until lunchtime the next day, when Lady Frances borrowed one of Mark's cars to drive to the nearest village and buy some cigarettes. She had only driven a few hundred yards when there was a huge explosion and the car burst into flames, careering off the road and into the stony mountainside. She was killed instantly.

Mark was devastated by the loss. The car was a 1962 Morgan Plus 8 Drop Head Coupé in midnight blue, one of about three or four left in the world, and it would be impossible to replace.

Jonathan Coe, *What a Carve Up!*, 1994.

« Peut-être la Grande-Bretagne était-elle en pleine récession » : allusion à la situation économique peu réjouissante dans laquelle se trouvait le pays en 1981, au moment où l'action se déroule.

1. Who? ....

2. Where? ....

3. When? ....

4. What happens? ....

5. Consequences: ....

SE TESTER

1 1. c – 2. c – 3. b – 4. a – 5. b – 6. c – 7. b – 8. b

S'ENTRAÎNER

2 1. His mother had a stroke ("four years ago", l. 9). 2. His father died ("a full month before Thérèse walked out on him" , l. 1-2). 3. Thérèse walked out on him. 4. He took Juliette out to Minnesota to live with his sister. 5. The lawyer found him. 6. He became rich ("money fell into his lap", l. 15).

OBJECTIF BAC

3 1. **Who?** Rich people ("select members of the aristocracy and business community", l. 2) attended a wedding ceremony and then the wedding party. It was the wedding of Mark and Lady Frances.

2. **Where?** First, in Britain, where the wedding took place, and then on the Riviera *(la Côte d'Azur)*, where Mark and Lady Frances had planned to begin ("were to begin", l. 9) their honeymoon *(lune de miel)*.

3. **When?** At a time when there was a recession in Britain. (That was in the 1980s.)

Chronology

- First day: the wedding took place. Mark and Lady Frances flew to Nice before the wedding party was over ("a lavish party which was still going strong [...] at four o'clock the next afternoon", l. 4-5). Mark and Lady Frances "had departed the revels early in the evening" (l. 7). Mark and Lady Frances arrived at Mark's villa "shortly after midnight", (l. 9-10).
- Second day ("the next day", l. 10): the explosion.

4. **What happens?** Mark and Lady Frances slept in very late and then Lady Frances borrowed one of Mark's cars to drive to the nearest village, but soon the car exploded. Lady Frances was killed and the car was completely destroyed ("it would be impossible to replace", l. 16-17). We know that there was an explosion, but we do not know what caused it.

5. **Consequences:** Mark was very shocked, very upset because the car was completely destroyed and impossible to replace ("Mark was devastated by the loss", l. 15). It seems that Mark was not upset about his wife's death (and that replacing her would not be a problem).

CHAPITRE

2 Répondre aux questions de compréhension

La réussite à l'épreuve de compréhension écrite au baccalauréat dépend d'une lecture attentive des questions de compréhension et d'une application rigoureuse des consignes. En outre, même si c'est votre compréhension du texte qui est évaluée, il faut soigner la rédaction des réponses qui doivent être données en anglais.

I Comprendre et appliquer les consignes

A Répondre à un exercice du type « vrai ou faux ? »

- Pour répondre à un exercice du type *true or false?* (parfois appelé *right or wrong?*), donnez votre réponse et justifiez votre choix en citant le texte *(Quote from the text)*, sans oublier les guillemets, ni le numéro de la ligne.

- Pour commencer, lisez avec la plus grande attention la phrase que vous devez confirmer *(true / right)* ou infirmer *(false / wrong)*. Relisez le passage auquel se rapporte la phrase. Relisez cette phrase **avant** d'inscrire votre réponse. La citation ne doit pas être trop longue et être pertinente. Au besoin, soulignez les groupes de mots particulièrement significatifs pour montrer au correcteur que vous n'avez pas répondu au hasard.

B Répondre à un QCM

- Si on vous propose un QCM (questionnaire à choix multiples / *multiple choice questionnaire*), cochez la case qui correspond à la bonne réponse *(Tick the right box / answer)*. Si vous devez cocher plusieurs cases, cela est précisé dans l'énoncé.

- D'abord, lisez très attentivement tous les choix proposés, puis relisez bien le passage concerné. Une nouvelle étude des choix proposés est souvent très utile avant de répondre.

C Compléter un texte lacunaire

- Si vous devez compléter un résumé ou un commentaire du texte (ou d'une partie du texte), faites-le uniquement avec des mots ou des phrases pertinents, directement tirés du texte.
- Si vous devez compléter le texte lacunaire avec vos propres mots, la consigne indique *in your own words*.

D Répondre à des questions « classiques »

Votre réponse doit correspondre strictement à la question posée : attention aux « débordements » et aux hors sujets. **Rédigez toujours** vos réponses, même si celles-ci doivent être brèves, en reformulant le plus possible le contenu du texte. Il faut prouver que vous avez compris celui-ci sans le répéter systématiquement. On peut vous demander de rédiger une réponse en un **nombre donné de mots**. Ce nombre est une exigence minimale. Pensez aussi à **gérer le temps** qui vous est imparti.

II Connaître le vocabulaire indispensable

Vous devez impérativement connaître le sens des mots et expressions suivants.

A Le texte et les personnages

an excerpt (from a book / a magazine...) / a passage (from...): un extrait tiré de...

throughout the excerpt: d'un bout à l'autre de l'extrait

the whole /həʊl/ passage / the entire /ɪnˈtaɪə/ passage is about... le passage tout entier parle de...

a sentence: une phrase ≠ a phrase: une expression

as implied in the opening sentence, ... comme le suggère la première phrase, ...

a paragraph; an account (of): un récit (de)

a summary of ; to sum up: un résumé ; résumer

Jane is present in the scene. ≠ Fred is absent from the scene. Jane assiste à la scène. ≠ Fred n'assiste pas à la scène.

B Le sens de la ponctuation et des mots

The punctuation **highlights** Bob's anxiety. La ponctuation souligne l'inquiétude de Bob.

The pronoun "she" **refers to** Liz. Le pronom *she* renvoie à Liz.

an intentional repetition: une répétition volontaire

The adverb "clearly" **occurs** /ə'kɜːz/ three times. L'adverbe *clearly* apparaît trois fois.

The verb "hiss" **is aimed at** rendering Lucy's anger. Le verbe *hiss* sert à exprimer la colère de Lucy.

The adjective "white" **evokes / symbolizes** Charlotte's innocence. L'adjectif *white* évoque / symbolise l'innocence de Charlotte.

Kay **is depicted as** a selfish mother. Kay est représentée comme une mère égoïste.

The emphasis /'emfəsɪs/ **on** the pronoun "I" **conveys** Nick's authority. L'emphase placée sur le pronom « *I* » montre bien l'autorité de Nick.

an exaggeration ; to exaggerate: une exagération ; exagérer

To say that Jo is strange is an understatement /'ʌndəˌsteɪtmənt/, Jo is raging mad! Dire que Jo est bizarre est un euphémisme, Jo est fou à lier !

C Le travail de l'auteur

The author /'ɔːθə/ **informs us that... / about...** L'auteur nous apprend que...

The writer **makes it clear that...** L'auteur montre clairement que...

The novelist **illustrates** Bill's happiness **with such words as** "joy" and "bliss". L'auteur illustre / exprime le bonheur de Bill avec des mots tels que « joie » et « béatitude ».

The writer **highlights / underlines / stresses / underscores** Tim's cruelty. L'écrivain souligne / insiste sur la cruauté de Tim.

The author **insists on** Julia's despair **by writing** two long sentences about her nightmares. L'auteur insiste bien sur / met en évidence le désespoir de Julia avec deux longues phrases sur ses cauchemars.

The reporter **aims to** explain the causes of the epidemic. L'intention du reporter est d'expliquer les causes de l'épidémie.

The journalist **ridicules** the dictator. Le journaliste ridiculise le dictateur.

III Être compris

Les correcteurs ont parfois bien du mal à comprendre ce qu'écrivent les élèves, non seulement à cause des fautes de grammaire et des lacunes lexicales, mais aussi à cause du manque de cohérence, de logique qui caractérise certaines copies.

A Maîtriser les mots de liaison

Pour que votre anglais soit naturel, utilisez les mots et les formules de liaison avec modération, uniquement quand ils sont utiles, et non pour faire du « remplissage ».

QUELQUES MOTS DE LIAISON

- moreover, furthermore: en outre • however: cependant • therefore: donc • consequently, as a result: par conséquent • thus: ainsi, de cette manière
- Attention à whereas. Utilisez plutôt while, bien plus naturel et plus facile à manipuler. Ed works hard while Ada is lazy. Ed travaille beaucoup alors que Ada est paresseuse.

B Éviter les clichés

Évitez d'utiliser les expressions ci-dessous. Ce sont des clichés qui agacent les correcteurs : *(to put it) in a nutshell ; to cut a long story short ; last but not least ; as a matter of fact ; in this world and age ; indeed.*

Utilisez plutôt : ***in short, in fact, today, it is true that...***

ATTENTION

On peut dire *according to the author* ou *according to him*, mais on ne dira en aucun cas ~~according to me~~. On dit : *(Personally,) I think / I suppose ; in my opinion...*

C Soigner la ponctuation

Rappelez-vous : ponctuation = sens. Comparez les phrases ci-dessous.

John says Alice is silly. John, says Alice, is silly.

Grandpa told us a story which was quite unusual. Grandpa told us a story, which was quite unusual.

Les mots sont les mêmes, l'ordre des mots est le même, et c'est la ponctuation qui fait la différence de sens.

RÉCAPITULONS

- La lecture attentive des questions de compréhension et le respect des consignes sont indispensables pour réussir l'épreuve.
- Il existe plusieurs types de questions : *true or false?*, texte lacunaire à compléter, QCM et questions plus classiques. Dans tous les cas, il faut éviter de répéter le texte, sauf si on vous le demande dans la consigne.
- Il faut mémoriser dès la classe de 1re un certain nombre de mots et expressions qui vous aideront à répondre avec précision et dans une langue soignée, même s'il s'agit d'une épreuve de compréhension.

Répondre aux différents types de questions

LA DÉMARCHE

- Je lis attentivement les questions pour bien appliquer les **consignes**.
- Je réponds en utilisant le **vocabulaire approprié** et en évitant de répéter le texte mot pour mot, sauf lorsque des citations sont explicitement demandées.

L'EXEMPLE COMMENTÉ

Après une lecture attentive du texte ci-dessous, vous lirez les questions ainsi que les réponses proposées en bleu en prenant bien garde aux remarques méthodologiques.

" She hadn't visited her family for five years except for three days at Christmas, that annual ritual of consanguinity which she had always dreaded. She was received with a scrupulous politeness and a strict adherence to accepted social norms which didn't hide the absence of real warmth or genuine affection. She didn't resent this – whatever she herself was bringing to the family, it wasn't love – but she wished there was some acceptable way of excusing herself from the visit. She suspected that the others felt the same but were inhibited by the need to observe social conventions. To have one's widowed and solitary mother for Christmas was accepted as a duty and, once established, couldn't be avoided without the risk of sly gossip or mild scandal. So punctiliously on Christmas Eve, by a train they had suggested as convenient, she would arrive at Basingstoke station to be met by Roger or Jennifer, her over-heavy case taken from her like the burden it was, and the annual ordeal would get underway.

sly: (here) secretive
burden: fardeau
ordeal: a difficult, painful experience

P. D. James, *The Murder Room*, 2003.

1. Say if the following statements are true or false and justify by quoting the text.

a. The main character enjoyed celebrating Christmas with her children.
False. "that annual ritual of consanguinity which she had always dreaded." (l. 2-3)

b. The main character's husband is dead.
True. "To have one's widowed and solitary mother for Christmas" (l. 9-10)

- Le verbe dread (redouter) et l'adjectif widowed (veuve) sont soulignés afin de bien montrer que ces mots sont très importants pour justifier la réponse.
- Notez également l'emploi des guillemets anglais (quotation marks) pour citer le texte, ainsi que la référence à la ligne du texte.

2. Fill in the blanks with words taken from the text.

The main character, who is the ...... of either Roger or Jennifer is expected to go to ...... for Christmas. But her family do not act out of ...... for her but only seem to respect social .... Therefore, she would like to find a good ...... to avoid visiting them.

The main character, who is the mother of either Roger or Jennifer is expected to go to Basingstoke for Christmas. But her family do not act out of love / affection for her but only seem to respect social norms / conventions. Therefore, she would like to find a good excuse to avoid visiting them.

Comme c'est le cas dans la deuxième phrase à deux endroits différents, il peut arriver que deux synonymes puissent compléter un même blanc. Il faudra alors choisir un seul mot.

3. How does the main character feel about visiting her family? Slightly embarrassed, depressed or guilty? Explain (60 words).

She is only slightly embarrassed. Although she knows that her family do not love her, she does not care. She is aware that she is not particularly fond of them either, that she does not bring them love when she visits them. She could be expected to be excited at the prospect of seeing her family again, but she is not. She feels, therefore, neither depressed nor guilty. (68 words)

- Le nombre de mots indiqué dans la consigne est en général un nombre minimal.
- Notez l'emploi de phrases complexes et d'un seul mot de liaison (*therefore*) à la fin du paragraphe.

SE TESTER QUIZ

1 Comprendre le vocabulaire des consignes

Cochez la traduction appropriée.

1. Pick out.
- ☐ **a.** Relevez.
- ☐ **b.** Donnez.

2. Quote.
- ☐ **a.** Expliquez.
- ☐ **b.** Citez.

3. Explain what the sentence implies.
- ☐ **a.** Expliquez ce que la phrase démontre.
- ☐ **b.** Expliquez ce que la phrase suggère.

4. Say who or what the pronoun refers to.
- ☐ **a.** Dites à qui ou à quoi le pronom renvoie.
- ☐ **b.** Dites ce que le pronom exprime.

5. How are the two characters related?
- ☐ **a.** Quel est le lien entre les deux personnages?
- ☐ **b.** Quel type de rapport entretiennent les deux personnages ?

6. Draw the main character's portrait.
- ☐ **a.** Dessinez le portrait du personnage principal.
- ☐ **b.** Dressez le portrait du personnage principal.

S'ENTRAÎNER

2 Rédiger ses réponses correctement

Imaginez les réponses aux questions ci-dessous en utilisant les éléments donnés en italiques.

1. Who is the narrator? (Name, job.) *young man - witnessed the crash - Sebastian Parks - dog-trainer*
2. In what country does the scene take place? *South Africa*
3. When exactly does the scene take place? *one cold night - March 2005*
4. Is the main character afraid at first? *No - not aware of the danger*

OBJECTIF BAC

3 Répondre aux questions de compréhension

Texte 1

Lisez ce texte intégralement au moins deux fois puis répondez aux questions.

“At the top of the ridge Jody was winded. He paused, puffing noisily. The blood pounded in his ears. Then he saw what he was looking for. Below, in one of the little clearings in the brush lay the red pony. In the distance, Jody could see the legs moving slowly and convulsively. And in a circle around him stood the buzzards, waiting for the moment of death they knew so well.

Jody leaped forward and plunged down the hill. The wet ground muffled his steps and the brush hid him. When he arrived, it was all over. The first buzzard sat on the pony's head and its beak had just risen dripping with dark eye fluid. Jody plunged into the circle like a cat. The black brotherhood arouse in a cloud, but the big one on the pony's head was too late. As it hopped along to take off, Jody caught its wing tip and pulled it down. It was nearly as big as he was. The free wing crashed into his face with the force of a club, but he hung on. The claws fastened on his legs and the wing elbows battered his head on either side. Jody groped blindly with his free hand. His finger found the neck of the struggling bird. The red eyes looked into his face, calm and fearless and fierce; the naked head turned from side to side. Then the beak opened and vomited a stream of putrefied fluid. Jody brought up his knee and fell on the great bird. He held the neck to the ground with one hand while his other found a piece of sharp white quarz. The first blow broke the beak sideways and black blood spurted from the twisted, leathery mouth corners. He struck again and missed. The red fearless eyes still looked at him, impersonal and unafraid and detached. He struck again and again, until the buzzard lay dead, until its head was red pulp. He was still beating the dead bird when Billy Buck pulled him off and held him tightly to calm his shaking.

Carl Tiflin wiped the blood from the boy's face with a red bandana. Jody was limp and quiet now. His father moved the buzzard with his toe. “Jody,” he explained, “the buzzard didn't kill the pony. Don't you know that?”

ridge: crête • winded: essoufflé • clearings in the brush: clairières dans les broussailles • leaped forward: fit un bond en avant • muffled his steps: amortissait le bruit de ses pas • beak: bec • its wing tip: l'extrémité de son aile • club: massue • claws: serres • blow: coup • limp: sans force

"I know it," Jody said wearily.

It was Billy Buck who was angry. He had lifted Jody in his arms, and had turned away to carry him home. But he turned back on Carl Tiflin. "Course he knows it," Billy said furiously. "Jesus Christ! man, can't you see how he'd feel about it?"

John Steinbeck, *The Red Pony*, 1933.

1. Give the names of the people present in the passage and, when possible, say how they are related.

2. Say if the statement is true or false and justify by quoting the text.
The birds had formed a circle around the pony to attack his carcass as soon as he was dead.

3. Pick out the sentence indicating that the pony has finally died.

4. "Jody jumped into the circle like a cat" (l. 12-13). What did the boy do that for?

5. **a.** What does the killing of the buzzard that Jody has managed to catch show about the boy's emotions? (40 words)

b. Is the buzzard depicted in a negative way? Explain by referring to the text. (40 words)

c. Was the killing of the buzzard entirely legitimate? Justify by referring to the text. (30 words)

d. What kind of father does Carl Tiflin seem to be? (60 words)

6. When John Steinbeck wrote this passage, how did he expect the readers to feel about it? Explain in your own words (80 words).

Texte 2

Lisez maintenant ce second texte et répondez aux questions 1 à 5.

" **Easing the Way in Therapy With the Aid of an Animal** by Jane E. Brody

A growing number of psychotherapists are using therapy animals to facilitate treatment, especially treatment of children with emotional, social and even physical problems.

Among the pioneers is Aubrey H. Fine, psychotherapist and professor at the California State Polytechnic University in Pomona, whose extensive successful use of therapy animals in treating children is documented in "The Handbook on Animal Assisted Therapy" (Elsevier/Academic Press, 2010).

As Dr. Fine describes one of his first and most inspiring cases, 5-year-old Diane was brought to him because she recoiled in fright from strangers, and though she spoke at home, she refused to speak to anyone else, including her kindergarten teacher.

A trained therapy dog named Puppy eventually broke the back of her selective mutism. Diane was petting Puppy, smiling and content, when Dr. Fine gave the dog a signal to walk away. Diane was crestfallen, and seeing the girl's distress, Dr. Fine told her that all she had to do to get the dog back was to say, "Puppy, come." Softly, the child said, "Puppy, come, please come, Puppy." That incident became the bridge Dr. Fine needed to help the child overcome her socially disabling problem.

He tells of another troubled child who finally began to speak about being physically abused when Dr. Fine told him that the misshapen therapy animal he was playing with had been rescued from an abusive home where it had been seriously injured. In another case in which a child was told where — and where not — to touch the therapy animal, the child opened up about being inappropriately touched, sexually abused, by a family member.

"Children are more likely to reveal inner thoughts to the therapist because the animal is right next to them and helps them express themselves," Dr. Fine said in an interview.

In early work in a social skills program for hyperactive children, Dr. Fine found that they could be more easily taught how to behave calmly if allowed to handle his pet gerbil. "I realized this approach can have a tremendous impact in teaching because it helps to change how we relate to other beings," he said.

The *New York Times*, March 14, 2011.

1. Who is Aubrey H. Fine (job, place of work, country)? He is described as being "among the pioneers" (l. 4). Explain in your own words why, and in what specific field he is a pioneer.

2. Say if these statements about Diane, "one of his first and most inspiring cases" (l. 8), are true or false. Justify by quoting the text.

a. Diane was a teenager when she met Aubrey H. Fine.

b. She didn't speak to people who were not immediate family.

c. She cried when she saw someone she didn't know.

3. What did Diane's treatment consist of? Fill in the blanks, using words and names from l. 12 to l. 18.

Diane was introduced to a dog called **(a)** ... . She was happy while **(b)** ... him and after the dog was told to walk away from her, her **(c)** ... was obvious. But when she was told to call the dog **(d)** ..., she did it. The dog had made it possible for **(e)** ... to help Diane **(f)** ... her selective mutism.

4. The article also mentions three instances of animal assisted therapy, one involving a "troubled child" who was "physically abused" (l. 19-20), another involving a child who was "sexually abused" (l. 24), and programs for hyperactive children (l. 28). For each example, say what the result of the therapy was. (70 words)

5. Choose the right equivalent for the words and phrases below.

a. "crestfallen" (l. 14)

- ☐ happy ☐ disconcerted ☐ furious

b. "Children are more likely to reveal inner thoughts" (l. 25)

- ☐ It's impossible for children to reveal what they really think.
- ☐ Children would like to reveal what they really think.
- ☐ Children are more disposed to reveal what they really think.

c. "we relate to other beings" (l. 31)

- ☐ We tell our story to other people.
- ☐ We communicate with other people.
- ☐ We play with other people.

Textes 1 et 2

Relisez les deux textes intégralement, puis répondez aux questions 1 et 2.

> Lors de l'examen, on pourra proposer, comme ci-dessous, des questions mettant en relation les deux textes.

1. What do the children mentioned in the article and Jody in *The Red Pony* (p. 27-28) have in common? (50 words)

2. In the passage from *The Red Pony*, which adult character could be associated with Dr. Fine? (50 words)

SE TESTER

1 1. a – 2. b – 3. b – 4. a – 5. a – 6. b

S'ENTRAÎNER

2 1. The narrator is a young man who witnessed the crash. His name is Sebastian Parks. He is a dog-trainer. 2. The scene is set in South Africa.
3. The scene takes place one cold night in March 2005.
4. No, (s)he is not afraid because (s)he is not aware of the danger.

OBJECTIF BAC

3 Proposition de corrigé

TEXTE 1

1. There is a boy, named Jody. Carl Tiflin is his father. There is another man, Billy Buck.

2. True. "And in a circle around him stood the buzzards, waiting for the moment of death they knew so well." (l. 6-7).

> Notez que c'est le pronom *him* et non *it* qui fait référence à l'animal. Ce poney est celui de Jody qui lui voue une grande affection.

3. "When he arrived it was all over." (l. 10) (it was all over : *c'était fini*).

4. Jody tried to frighten off the buzzards so they would fly away and leave the pony alone. He did not want them to touch the pony's dead body.

5. **a.** The killing of the buzzard is extremely violent. It shows that the boy, who obviously loved the pony very much, was extremely upset and angry. Not only because the pony was dead, but also because the buzzards had been looking forward to his death. Jody was so upset that he went on beating the buzzard after it was dead. (59 words)
b. The buzzard is not at all depicted in a negative way. Until the end, the bird shows dignity and great courage. It is a powerful bird ("The free wing crashed into his face with the force of a club", l. 15-16). The buzzard's eyes show that it is brave ("The red eyes looked into his face, calm and fearless and fierce", l. 19, "The red fearless eyes still looked at him, impersonal and unafraid and detached", l. 25-26). It seems that the buzzard is defiant, that it is challenging Jody. (46 words)

Notez que les citations ne doivent pas être comptabilisées dans le nombre de mots exigé.

c. Jody's misery and anger are understandable. However, buzzards or no buzzards the pony would have died. Carl Tiflin explains this to his son, and Jody knows that his father is right: "'Jody,' he explained, 'the buzzard didn't kill the pony. Don't you know that?' 'I know it,' Jody said wearily. (l. 32), "'Course he knows it,' Billy said furiously." (l. 34-35). (32 words)
d. Carl Tiflin does not understand why the sight of the hungry buzzards upset his son so much. He simply does not understand that Jody loved the pony. The father says "the buzzard didn't kill the pony" (l. 31). The use of the article "the" for both the buzzard and the pony shows that, in Tiflin's view, the two animals are the same. As Billy Buck points out angrily, Carl Tiflin is pathetic *(lamentable)* here. And it is Billy, not Tiflin, who carries Jody in his arms. (78 words)

6. The passage is very poignant. It contains three disturbing events: the pony's death, the massacre of the buzzard, and Carl Tiflin's reaction. Tiflin's failure to see his son's suffering makes us feel even more sorry for the boy. The passage is very violent too. Nature is violent. Jody's killing of the bird is pitiless, and it is cruel because the buzzard only behaved in a natural way. The details about the killing of the bird are meant to make the reader feel uncomfortable. And, of course, there is emotional cruelty and violence about Tiflin's reaction. Only a very insensitive reader can remain indifferent to the scene. (106 words)

Texte 2

1. Aubrey H. Fine is a psychotherapist and professor at the California State Polytechnic University in Pomona, in the USA. He is considered a pioneer because he was one of the first psychotherapists who used animals to treat troubled children. He even wrote a book about this type of therapy.

2. a. False. "5-year-old Diane was brought to him" (l. 8-9) and "her kindergarten teacher" (l. 10-11)
b. True. "though she spoke at home, she refused to speak to anyone else." (l. 9-10)
c. False. "she recoiled in fright from strangers" (l. 9)

3. **(a)** Puppy **(b)** petting **(c)** distress **(d)** back **(e)** Dr. Fine / Fine **(f)** overcome

4. The "troubled child" (l. 19) managed to tell Dr. Fine that he was ill-treated after seeing an animal which had also been the victim of physical cruelty and was consequently deformed ("misshapen", l. 20). The second child was able to speak about being sexually abused by a relative when he was told he was only allowed to touch certain parts of the animal's body. Hyperactive children could calm down when holding a gerbil, which is a small animal. (71 words)

5. a. disconcerted

b. Children are more disposed to reveal what they really think.

c. We communicate with other people.

TEXTES 1 ET 2

1. Jody, a fictional character, and Dr. Fine's young patients gain a lot from their exchanges with animals. The pony's death is a terrible loss for Jody because it must have given him the warmth his father was unable to give him. Like Jody, the troubled children mentioned in the article can enjoy a better quality of life thanks to the reassuring presence of animals. (64 words)

2. Billy Buck could be associated with Dr. Fine as he has understood how precious the pony was to Jody. He is the one who tries to soothe the child by taking him in his arms. Like Dr. Fine, he has understood that a child can benefit from being in contact with an animal. (53 words)

CHAPITRE

3 Écrire la suite d'un texte

Au baccalauréat, on peut vous demander d'écrire la suite d'un texte. Si on vous donne des indications ou des consignes plus précises, respectez-les bien. Sinon, appliquez-vous à reproduire l'esprit du texte de départ : par exemple, ne transformez pas une situation grave en une situation légère.

I Les consignes

Identifiez le type de travail qu'on attend de vous. Si on vous donne des consignes, repérez les mots clés qui signalent les pistes à suivre, comme, par exemple, la mise en valeur d'une attitude, d'une réaction, d'un sentiment.

- ***Write a sequel to the text / the narrative.*** Écrivez la suite du texte / du récit. Pas de consignes particulières : écrivez une suite qui respecte les caractéristiques du récit initial.
- ***Write a happy ending to the narrator's account*** **(récit)** ***of the incident.*** Ici, il faudra vous focaliser sur l'incident et vous assurer qu'il se termine bien. Cependant, ne trahissez pas l'esprit du texte. Attention aux retournements de situation peu vraisemblables.
- ***Suppose that Jane makes up her mind to leave. Imagine her angry thoughts as she walks home.*** Ici, ce n'est pas à vous de décider si Jane part ou non. Elle part, et elle est en colère : respectez bien la consigne.

II Préparez-vous

A La compréhension du texte

La qualité de votre devoir dépendra de celle de votre anglais, mais aussi de votre compréhension du texte de départ : la situation, son éventuelle évolution, l'identité et la psychologie des personnages, les liens qui les unissent.

Avant de commencer à rédiger la suite d'un récit, relisez très attentivement le texte et surtout la fin, pour savoir exactement à partir de quelle matière vous allez intervenir.

B Le narrateur

Vous allez devoir vous glisser dans la peau du narrateur. Qui est-il ? Que dit-il ? Vous devrez respecter la place qu'il occupe dans le texte de départ et la façon dont il formule son récit. Pour rédiger une suite cohérente, posez-vous les questions suivantes :

- A-t-on quelque indication sur son identité (sexe, âge, profession, etc.) ?
- Est-ce l'un des personnages du texte, est-ce un témoin ? Est-ce un narrateur omniscient (qui sait tout de la situation et des personnages) ?
- Que privilégie-t-il ? Une atmosphère (le temps, un paysage, une habitation) ? La psychologie d'un ou de plusieurs personnages ? Une relation humaine ? La nature d'une situation ? Son évolution ? Le suspense ?
- Comment, dans le texte, décrit-il la situation, les personnages ? Est-il bienveillant, critique, féroce, neutre ?
- Comment écrit-il ? Cette question est importante car vous devez écrire comme lui.

– Si son récit est à la première personne *(I)*, écrivez à la première personne. S'il est à la troisième personne (*he, she*, éventuellement *it* ou *they*), utilisez comme lui la troisième personne.

– La plupart des récits sont au prétérit, mais les récits au présent ne sont pas si rares. Conservez le temps utilisé dans le texte de départ.

– Le niveau de langue est également important. Si le narrateur emploie quelques formules argotiques, vous pouvez vous permettre de faire de même, **sans en abuser**. En revanche, si le style est soutenu tout au long du texte, il vous faudra choisir des structures adaptées.

ATTENTION !
Veillez bien à la concordance des temps (→ p. 182-188).

III Votre récit

A Quelques précautions

- Faites toujours un **brouillon** pour contrôler l'évolution du récit et vous orienter vers une conclusion en harmonie avec ce qui précède.
- Gardez en mémoire le **nombre de mots demandé** de façon à ne pas écrire une suite déséquilibrée. Respectez le nombre de mots et n'oubliez pas de l'indiquer entre parenthèses à la fin de votre travail.
- Soignez la **ponctuation**. Une ponctuation fantaisiste peut vous rendre incompréhensible (→ p. 23).

> He spoke to the secretary, who was angry-looking.
> Il s'adressa à la secrétaire, laquelle avait l'air de mauvaise humeur.
>
> ≠ He spoke to the secretary who was angry-looking.
> Il s'adressa à la secrétaire qui avait l'air de mauvaise humeur (et pas à une autre secrétaire).

• Une phrase se termine par un point, il n'y a jamais de virgule en tête de ligne.

• Les points d'exclamation traduisent une émotion : assurez-vous qu'ils sont justifiés.

• En outre, n'abusez pas des mots entre guillemets pour exprimer que vous n'êtes pas tout à fait satisfait de votre choix lexical. Il vaut mieux essayer de trouver une meilleure solution que de mettre en valeur un manque de votre part !

B La rédaction du récit

- Pour **débuter votre récit**, il n'est pas nécessaire de recopier la dernière phrase du récit *(account / narrative)* de départ. Poursuivez-le de façon aussi naturelle que possible, sans interruption ni changement de narrateur.
- La **progression de la narration** doit être visible ; faites des paragraphes bien distincts.
- Vous pouvez insérer ponctuellement un **dialogue** entre les personnages mais n'oubliez pas que la ponctuation d'un dialogue en anglais répond à des règles précises, différentes d'un dialogue en français (→ p. 45).
- Vous pouvez utiliser des **mots et locutions « de liaison »** mais avec modération, sinon votre récit ne sera pas naturel.

La **fin de votre récit** doit être cohérente. Elle dépend du texte de départ et de l'évolution que lui a donnée votre propre texte. Elle peut dépendre aussi des consignes.

ATTENTION !
Ne bâclez pas la fin de votre récit : venant en dernier, elle peut beaucoup influencer le correcteur.

RÉCAPITULONS

- Lorsqu'on doit écrire la suite d'un récit, il faut tenir compte du **texte de départ** et des **consignes** particulières s'il y en a.
- Il faut adopter le **point de vue** et le **niveau de langue du narrateur**.
- Il faut s'assurer de la **cohérence** de son propre récit.

Se préparer à rédiger

LA DÉMARCHE

- Je dois suivre les **consignes** et respecter le **contenu** et le **ton du texte d'origine**.
- Je soigne la **structure** de mon récit ainsi que l'**expression**.

L'EXEMPLE COMMENTÉ

Le texte ci-dessous est le récit d'origine.

Le narrateur est censé être Sigmund Freud, le fondateur de la psychanalyse. La scène se passe pendant une séance de psychanalyse.

“ One of her retractations related to her affair with A., the student whom she had loved in St Petersburg. So far, she had told me only trivial facts about him: such as that he was a student of philosophy, of wealthy and conservative background, a few years older than she, etc. She stuck to her story that it had been a “white” relationship. I was struck by the adjective she used, and asked her what she associated with the word “white”. She said it conjured up the sails of a yacht; and it seemed reasonable to suppose that she was recalling her father's yacht. But one should never jump to conclusions in psychoanalysis: she said she was thinking instead of one weekend in Petersburg when she and other members of the political group, including of course A., went out sailing in the Gulf. [...] She had never felt so much in love with A., and he was tender towards her, and respectful as always. They had to share a cabin, but he never once tried to touch her; their consciences remained as white as the sails, or as the white nights.

She was nevertheless fumbling with her crucifix, and her face wore an expression of sorrow.

D.M. Thomas, *The White Hotel*, 1981.

La patiente est revenue sur ce qu'elle avait dit lors d'une séance précédente.

Imagine what really happened with A. (250 words)

POUR VOUS AIDER

Il s'agit donc d'imaginer ce qui s'est réellement passé entre la patiente et le personnage désigné par la lettre A.

■ Il faut **rassembler les informations sur le narrateur qui apparaissent dans le texte d'origine :** ici, c'est l'un des deux personnages présents dans la scène. Censé être le fondateur de la psychanalyse, il rend compte des propos d'une patiente, lesquels sont essentiels pour la rédaction de la suite du passage. Comme dans le roman, le narrateur emploiera le pronom « *I* » pour se désigner, et « *she* », pour la jeune femme.

■ Il faut **garder en mémoire certains aspects du texte.**
- Le *past perfect* (l. 2), nous apprend que la patiente et A. ont vécu une idylle maintenant terminée.
- La dernière phrase de l'extrait montre bien que l'évocation de la croisière en compagnie de A. trouble la jeune femme, la rend triste. Le crucifix qu'elle tripote nerveusement peut être un indice de culpabilité. Peut-être porte-elle la culpabilité d'un incident douloureux. On est aussi en droit de penser que sa relation avec A. ne fut pas aussi innocente qu'elle le prétend. Peut-être même que A. ne l'a jamais aimée, ou l'a quittée dans des circonstances éprouvantes.
- On fera très attention aux temps des verbes (chronologie des événements).

■ **Exemple de suite du récit**

And then, she burst into tears and said that she needed to free herself from a terrible secret.
When she regained her composure, she confessed that one night, on the yacht, A. had admitted that although he had a lot of affection for her, he had never really loved her. He went on to say that he had agreed to go sailing with the group because he yearned to be with B., her closest friend, and for no other reason. And as he did not feel confident enough to do it himself, he wanted her to tell B. how much he loved her. He even expected her to give B. a letter telling her to meet him at the hotel the next day.
She was in a state of shock and felt as if she was going to faint. She was too weak to scream or cry, yet perhaps because she was in such a daze she promised to deliver the message.
But she never did. She had no reason to, after all. Instead, she told him that she had spoken to B., that B. had burst out laughing and torn his letter into tiny pieces without even reading it, for B. felt nothing but contempt for him. A. did not say a word. He walked away and they never spoke again.
Two weeks later, she learnt that A. had agreed to marry Olga, his short fat bad-tempered first cousin. He had signed a contract with misery and unhappiness. His life was ruined. She had ruined it. (257 words)

SE TESTER QUIZ

1 Différencier les niveaux de langue

Cochez celle des deux phrases écrite dans le registre le plus soutenu.

1. ☐ **a.** However silly he may be, everybody likes him.
   ☐ **b.** He may be silly, but everybody likes him.

2. ☐ **a.** Never had she told him the truth.
   ☐ **b.** She had never told him the truth.

3. ☐ **a.** No sooner had we left than it started to rain.
   ☐ **b.** As soon as we left, it started to rain.

4. ☐ **a.** He's got to pay the rent.
   ☐ **b.** He has to pay the rent.

5. ☐ **a.** It is crucial that he should be here.
   ☐ **b.** It is crucial for him to be here.

6. ☐ **a.** I dunno. I've never seen them.
   ☐ **b.** I don't know. I've never seen them.

7. ☐ **a.** Had we known, we would have spoken to her.
   ☐ **b.** If we had known we would have spoken to her.

8. ☐ **a.** You had better stop behaving like this.
   ☐ **b.** You would be well advised to stop behaving like this.

S'ENTRAÎNER

2 Utiliser la ponctuation qui convient

Rétablissez la ponctuation qui a été supprimée dans ce texte.

Penelope, qui a à peine treize ans, a été invitée à faire du camping par les parents d'une camarade de classe. Juliet et Eric sont les parents de Penelope.

" Juliet was in favor of this Penelope had been at Torrance House for only one year [...] and it pleased Juliet that she had already made so firm a friend and been accepted readily by the friend's family also she was going camping something that regular children did and that Juliet as a child had never had a chance to do [...]

Eric was apprehensive about the whole idea he thought Penelope was too young he didn't like her going on a holiday with people he knew so little about and now that she went to boarding school they saw too little of her as it was so why should that time be shortened
Juliet had another reason she simply wanted Penelope out of the way for the first couple of weeks of the summer holidays because the air was not clear between herself and Eric.

Alice Munro, *Runaway: Stories*, 2004.

OBJECTIF BAC

3 Préparer l'écriture d'une suite de texte

Lisez le texte puis répondez aux questions pour amorcer l'écriture d'une suite.

" She is overtaken by a sensation of unbeing. There is no other word for it. Standing beside her ticking car, facing Mrs Latch's garage (the plaster squirrels throw long shadows), she is no one; she is nothing. It seems, briefly, that by going to the hotel she has slipped out of her life, and this driveway, this garage, are utterly strange to her. She has been away. [...] She has gone to the hotel in secret, the way she might go to meet a lover. She stands, holding her car keys and her purse, staring at Mrs Latch's garage. The door, painted white, has a little green-shuttered window in it, as if the garage were a miniature house attached to the larger house. Laura's breathing is suddenly labored. She's slightly dizzy – it seems she might stumble and collapse onto Mrs Latch's smooth concrete drive. She considers getting back into her car, and driving away again. She forces herself to go forward. She reminds herself: she has to retrieve her child, take him home, and finish assembling her husband's birthday dinner. She has to do those ordinary things.

Michael Cunningham, *The Hours*, 1998.

overtaken: envahie • plaster squirrels: écureuils en plâtre • green-shuttered: aux volets verts • labored: difficile • is dizzy: a le vertige • stumble: trébucher • retrieve: aller chercher

1. The narrator

What type of narrator tells the story? Can we deduce anything about the narrator's identity and personality?

2. Keys to the sequel

Which of the following are plausible sequels?

a. Laura rings Mrs Latch's door-bell, picks up her child and drives home.

b. Laura stands a little longer outside Mrs Latch's house.

c. Laura can't do "those ordinary things" and drives away.

d. Laura drives back to the hotel to meet her lover.

3. How should the sequel be written?

a. Does the narrator comment on Laura's state of mind, or does he describe it?

b. Can your sequel contain descriptions?

c. What personal pronoun should be used? What tense?

d. In what register should the sequel be written?

SE TESTER

1 1. a – 2. a – 3. a – 4. b – 5. a – 6. b – 7. a – 8. b

S'ENTRAÎNER

2 Juliet was in favor of this. Penelope had been at Torrance House for only one year (,) [...] and it pleased Juliet that she had already made so firm a friend and been accepted readily by the friend's family. Also she was going camping, / – / (something that regular children did, / – /) and that Juliet, as a child, had never had a chance to do. [...]

Eric was apprehensive about the whole idea. He thought Penelope was too young. He didn't like her going on a holiday with people he knew so little about. And now that she went to boarding school they saw too little of her as it was, / – so why should that time be shortened?

Juliet had another reason – / : she simply wanted Penelope out of the way for the first couple of weeks of the summer holidays (,) because the air was not clear between herself and Eric.

OBJECTIF BAC

3 1. The narrator knows everything about Laura: what she did, what she is doing, her feelings. The narrator is omniscient. We do not know anything at all about "him". "He" does not exist as a character, the only reason why he exists in the book is to tell the story.

2. **a. b. c.** Laura does not have a lover waiting for her in a hotel: "She has gone to the hotel in secret, the way she might go to meet a lover." (l. 5-6) It is a comparison, there is no lover.

3. **a.** The author describes Laura's state of mind. He shows that she is not feeling well, that she is very depressed, but he never comments on this. He is neither sorry nor critical, he is neutral. You should write your sequel in a neutral way too, without judging Laura, without saying how sorry you feel for her.

b. The sequel can contain short descriptions. In the original text there are a few descriptions which highlight Laura's inability to connect with reality.

c. The narrative should be written in third person singular (she) and in the present tense, as in the excerpt.

d. The sequel should be written in standard / formal English.

CHAPITRE

4 Écrire un dialogue

Au baccalauréat, on peut vous demander de rédiger un dialogue à partir d'un texte. Il faut très bien connaître ce texte et, dans votre dialogue, en respecter les caractéristiques, tant au niveau du contenu que du style. Il faut aussi lire l'énoncé du sujet avec la plus grande attention car le contexte du dialogue (lieu, moment, personnages) y est la plupart du temps précisé.

I Les questions préalables à la rédaction

Avant d'entamer la rédaction d'un dialogue, **analysez précisément le contenu de la consigne** et posez-vous les questions suivantes.

A Où et quand la scène doit-elle avoir lieu ?

- Si l'endroit où le dialogue doit se dérouler est le même que dans le texte, respectez-en les caractéristiques. Mais attention, on peut vous demander de déplacer la scène.
- Repérez le moment de la journée, la saison ou l'époque. Attention aux anachronismes : n'introduisez pas un appareil photo numérique *(a digital camera)* ou un téléphone portable *(a mobile phone / a cellphone)* dans le monde des années 1920.

B Quelles sont les caractéristiques des interlocuteurs ?

Respectez leurs traits psychologiques, et, si nécessaire, physiques, de même que la manière dont ils agissent dans le texte de départ. Par exemple, un personnage odieux a peu de raisons de devenir sympathique ; une dispute au sujet d'un héritage a peu de raisons de se transformer en conflit politique.

C Comment faire parler les personnages ?

- C'est le texte de départ qui détermine la façon dont les personnages doivent s'exprimer dans votre dialogue.

L'âge, le milieu social, la situation dans laquelle ils se trouvent, leurs émotions, le statut de leur(s) interlocuteur(s) sont autant de données qu'il faut respecter : ne faites pas parler un adulte bon-chic-bon-genre comme un chef de gang, ou un jeune qui s'adresse à un copain comme s'il parlait au proviseur de son lycée.

- Là encore, méfiez-vous des anachronismes : ne faites pas employer à des personnages des années 60 un argot contemporain.

D Quelles fonctions de communication employer ?

Prenons le sujet suivant : *After her first meeting with John, Cynthia meets her best friend in a café. Imagine their conversation.* On peut choisir d'exprimer soit la déception et la désapprobation, soit l'enthousiasme de Cynthia. Quant à sa meilleure amie, elle emploiera probablement des expressions traduisant l'encouragement.

II La rédaction du dialogue

A La ponctuation

Ponctuez votre dialogue « à l'anglaise ». Comparez la présentation du même dialogue (guillemets, tirets) en français et en anglais.

Extrait de *Le Grand Meaulnes* d'Alain-Fournier (1913)	**Traduction en anglais de cet extrait** (Frank Davison, Oxford University Press, 1959)
Cette fois, le jeune homme salua, en disant très bas : « Voulez-vous me pardonner ? – Je vous pardonne, dit-elle gravement. Mais il faut que je rejoigne les enfants, puisqu'ils sont les maîtres aujourd'hui. Adieu. »	This time the young man bowed, and said in a low voice: "Will you forgive me?" "I forgive you," she said gravely. "But I must get back to the children; it's they who are giving orders today. Good-bye."

B Les verbes introducteurs

Ne vous contentez pas du verbe *say*. Utilisez aussi des verbes qui rendent bien la façon de parler des personnages.

ZOOM

Quelques verbes introducteurs utiles

add : ajouter
admit : admettre, avouer
answer : répondre
ask : demander
choke : s'étrangler, dire qqch. d'une voix étranglée
confess : avouer
exclaim : s'exclamer
falter : bredouiller
hesitate : hésiter
hiss : dire qqch. d'une voix sifflante
implore : implorer, supplier
inquire : se renseigner
mutter : marmonner
reply : répliquer
scream : crier, hurler (son aigu ou perçant)
shout : crier
stammer : balbutier
stutter : bégayer
suggest : suggérer, proposer
venture : se hasarder à dire
whisper : chuchoter
yell : hurler

C Les adverbes et compléments de manière

Ils enrichissent l'emploi de *say* et des verbes mentionnés ci-dessus (→ p. 166-167).

ZOOM

Quelques adverbes utiles

angrily
anxiously : avec inquiétude
arrogantly
bitterly : d'un ton amer
calmy
cheerfully : sur un ton gai, joyeux
enthusiastically
furiously
hesitantly
impatiently
imploringly
joyfully
kindly : gentiment
miserably : sur un ton malheureux
nervously
proudly
reproachfully
scornfully : sur un ton méprisant
softly
suspiciously : d'un ton soupçonneux
tersely : sèchement

D La variété des formulations

Il est souhaitable d'enrichir votre texte avec différentes formulations. Observez les mots en gras dans les lignes suivantes.

"You never loved me." She **spoke** bitterly now.

"You love your daddy, don't you?" His **voice** was soft and dangerous.

"Come along!" she **said in a** cheerful **tone**.

III L'authenticité de la langue orale

On ne parle pas de la même façon que l'on écrit : votre dialogue doit sonner juste, il doit traduire le naturel et la spontanéité qui caractérisent toute conversation.

A Le niveau de langue

C'est la situation et le rapport entre les interlocuteurs qui déterminent le choix du niveau de langue. Ainsi, spontanéité ne signifie pas nécessairement familiarité. Par exemple, les expressions *I wanna (I want to), I gotta (I've got to)* ou *I'm gonna (I'm going to)* ne sont justifiées que si les consignes précisent que les locuteurs doivent parler une langue particulièrement relâchée. Évitez les expressions vulgaires, même s'il en apparaît dans le texte.

B Les formes réduites

Dans un dialogue, privilégiez les formes réduites des verbes et des auxiliaires (*don't, isn't, wouldn't*, etc.). N'utilisez la forme pleine *not* que si vous souhaitez créer un effet d'emphase (insistance).

I did not smoke! (*Not* est alors fortement accentué.)
Ce n'est pas vrai. / Tu te trompes. Je n'ai pas fumé !

C La mise en relief

À l'oral, on met fréquemment un ou plusieurs mots en relief simplement par l'intonation. À l'écrit, on peut souligner le(s) mot(s) concerné(s).

"You are exaggerating again!" "I'm not exaggerating! You are!"
« Tu exagères, une fois de plus ! – Ce n'est pas moi qui exagère ! C'est toi ! »

D Les réponses brèves et les *tags* (→ p. 107)

- Prenons la question : *"Did you see Charlie yesterday?"*

On préférera la réponse *"Yes, I did"* (ou *"No, I didn't"*) à un simple *"Yes"* (ou *"No"*).

- *So* et *not* dans les réponses brèves

  "Was Matilda present at the scene?" "(Yes,) I think so."

  "Has she spoken to Inspector Gates yet?" "(No,) I don't think so."

  "Has she recovered from the shock?" "I hope so."

  "Was she injured in the attack?" "I hope not."

- Les réponses brèves ne sont pas les seuls éléments qui dynamisent un dialogue. Un ou deux *tags* seront les bienvenus, mais il faut les utiliser avec modération, sinon le résultat risque d'être très artificiel.
- La construction des *tags* est généralement la suivante : lorsque le premier verbe (ou auxiliaire de modalité) est à la forme affirmative, l'auxiliaire du *tag* est à la forme négative et c'est l'inverse quand le premier élément est à la forme négative. Les *tags* se terminent par un pronom personnel ou par *there*.

  Liz worked (+) for you, didn't (–) she?

  Andrew can't (–) drive, can (+) he?

  There isn't (–) any salt, is (+) there?

Avec les adverbes négatifs *(never)* ou semi-négatifs *(hardly, hardly ever)*, l'auxiliaire est affirmatif dans le *tag*.

  You've never met her, have you?

  She hardly knew him, did she?

NOTEZ AUSSI :

Let's dance, shall we?
I'm late, aren't I?
Hurry up, will you?
Don't be late, will you?

RÉCAPITULONS

- Le contenu du dialogue à écrire dépend du texte d'origine. Il faut en respecter les **caractéristiques** et lire les **consignes** dans le détail.
- La **ponctuation** du dialogue diffère en anglais et en français.
- L'**authenticité** du dialogue dépend de votre capacité à employer des expressions tirées de la langue orale, en évitant la vulgarité.

Se préparer à l'écriture d'un dialogue

LA DÉMARCHE

- Je dois suivre les **consignes** et tenir compte du contenu du **texte d'origine**.
- Je dois employer des structures propres à la **langue orale** ainsi qu'une **ponctuation** appropriée.

L'EXEMPLE COMMENTÉ

Le texte ci-dessous est le texte d'origine. Il donne la situation de départ.

Bernard Walsh, un Anglais timide et très croyant, et son père, lui aussi très croyant, sont à Honolulu, où ils sont venus retrouver une parente. Le père de Bernard vient de se faire renverser par une conductrice en robe rouge.

"Who's the owner of the car?" said the second policeman. "I am," said the woman in the red dress. "The old guy stepped right out in front of me. I didn't have a prayer." The expression seemed to trigger a reaction in Mr Walsh, who began to mutter the Act of Contrition under his breath. "Oh my God, I am heartily sorry for all my sins..." Kneeling beside him, Bernard felt his hand rising by conditioned reflex to perform the gesture of absolution, and, embarrassed, converted it into a soothing stroke of the old man's brow. "No need for that, Daddy," he said. "You're going to be all right." He turned to the policeman: "He looked the wrong way, I'm afraid. We drive on the left, you see, in England."

A man in a neat lightweight suit stepped forward and said to Bernard, "Take my advice – make no admissions." He took a card from his wallet and offered it to Bernard. "I'm a lawyer. Be glad to act for you on a contingency basis. No fees unless the suit is successful."

"Keep your nose out of this, mister," said the woman in the red dress, snatching the card and tearing it in half. "You people make me sick, you're like vultures."

"That's actionable," said the lawyer calmly.

"Take it easy, lady," said the policeman.

converted it into a soothing stroke: transforma ce geste en une caresse
make no admissions: ne faites aucune concession
on a contingency basis = L'avocat ne percevra des honoraires *(fees)* que s'il gagne le procès *(suit / lawsuit)*.
actionable: passible de poursuites

"Listen, I'm driving along the road, minding my own business, and suddenly this old man throws himself under my wheels, out of nowhere. Now I'm being threatened with a lawsuit. And you tell me to take it easy. Jesus!"
"Jesus mercy, Mary help," Mr Walsh muttered.
"Tell them," the woman appealed to Bernard. "You said it wasn't my fault, right?"
"Yes," said Bernard.
"My client is in shock," said the lawyer. "He doesn't know what he is saying."
"He's not your client, asshole," said the woman in the red dress.
"Where's this ambulance?" said Bernard. His voice sounded plaintive even to his own ears. He envied the woman her anger and her expletives.

David Lodge, *Paradise News*, 1991.

expletives: franc-parler

While Mr Walsh is being driven to hospital, his son, Bernard, and the American woman who was driving the car try to get rid of the lawyer who finally gives up. Write the conversation (150 words, +/-10%).

POUR VOUS AIDER

Les points clés de la consigne sont les suivants :
- While Mr Walsh is being driven to hospital: le moment de l'action
- Bernard, the American woman, the lawyer: les personnages
- (the lawyer) who finally gives up: la situation finale

■ Le dialogue aura lieu **dans la rue**, comme dans le texte de départ : les trois personnages n'ont pas quitté le lieu de l'accident. De plus, la scène se passe **de nos jours**.

■ Avant de rédiger le dialogue il faut réfléchir à **la façon de faire parler** Bernard, la conductrice et l'avocat et à **leurs motivations** (psychologie, intérêts respectifs, nationalités, cultures). Ensuite, il faut se demander quelles **fonctions de communication** peuvent être mises en œuvre. Enfin, il est nécessaire de noter au brouillon la progression du dialogue sous forme de **plan**.

Les personnages

– **Bernard** est un homme discret et mesuré. Son père vient de se faire renverser par une voiture mais ce dernier n'est pas gravement blessé et Bernard ne manifeste aucune colère à l'égard de la conductrice. Il est anglais et n'est pas habitué à l'omniprésence des avocats ; il est même étonné par l'insistance avec laquelle l'avocat lui propose ses services.
Dans le dialogue, il devra s'exprimer avec retenue.

– **La conductrice** est américaine et a donc l'habitude de voir des avocats pousser les gens à intenter des procès pour un oui ou pour un non. Contrairement à Bernard, elle a une forte personnalité et ne mâche pas ses mots.
Dans le dialogue, elle devra être directive et parler avec assurance. Même s'il lui arrive d'être très vulgaire *(asshole)*, il n'est pas souhaitable de l'être dans votre copie.

– **L'avocat** est également autoritaire et pressant. Il s'est certainement rendu compte que Bernard est anglais et que c'est donc une proie facile.
Dans le dialogue, ce personnage fera tout pour convaincre Bernard de poursuivre la conductrice en justice et pour empêcher celle-ci de protester.

Le **ton du texte d'origine** n'est pas vraiment sérieux étant donné l'absence de gravité de l'accident et le décalage entre la situation et la réaction des personnages.
Il faudra adopter le même ton humoristique dans votre dialogue.

Les **fonctions de communications** à privilégier pourraient être les suivantes :

– **Bernard :** la désapprobation, le regret, le reproche modéré. Il est étonné par l'attitude de l'avocat et ne comprend pas les raisons qui le poussent à proposer ses services. Il va donc tenter de s'en débarrasser, mais sans trop le brusquer.

– **La conductrice :** le reproche, la critique, l'exaspération, la mise en garde. Elle est énervée en raison de l'accident et ne veut pas avoir de problèmes supplémentaires. Le caractère conciliant de Bernard peut également augmenter son agacement.

– **L'avocat :** le conseil, la suggestion, la détermination. Il veut profiter de la situation : Bernard est ému par l'accident de son père et doit se sentir perdu. L'avocat se présente en sauveur. Grâce à son métier, il connaît la rhétorique, d'où son insistance.

– Lorsque Bernard et la conductrice auront réussi à se débarrasser de l'avocat : la joie et le soulagement.

- **Proposition de dialogue :**

"Sir, I shall not let this woman deprive you of your rights," the lawyer exclaimed. "This is America, this is the country of Rights, and you have the right to sue a woman who seriously injured your father."

"Well," Bernard murmured, "isn't that going a little too far?"

"What the devil do you think you're doing?" shouted the woman at the top of her voice. "You are nothing but a crook. This gentleman said he would not sue me, and by the way, if anyone must be sued it should be his own father..."

"Well, he's English and he's an old man, and he..." Bernard ventured.

"Yes, he's an old man, precisely," interrupted the lawyer, "and the medical costs will be horrendous. Why should he pay for them?"

"I'm warning you," said the woman in a voice that meant trouble, "the police are still here and if you don't..."

"OK, OK, I wanted to do my duty, that's all. I wish you good luck, sir. Goodbye."

"Phew! I'm so glad he's gone," said Bernard.

"So am I!" said the woman triumphantly. I'm so relieved. Let's celebrate, shall we?"

(188 words)

Notez dans la dernière phrase l'emploi d'une réponse brève *(So am I!)*, d'un adverbe décrivant le ton de la conductrice *(triumphantly)* et d'un *tag (shall we?)*.

SE TESTER QUIZ

1 Identifier les fonctions de communication

Cochez les deux phrases correspondant à la fonction de communication indiquée.

1. Conseil :
- ☐ **a.** You ought to have a cup a tea.
- ☐ **b.** Would you like a cup a tea?
- ☐ **c.** You'd better have a cup of tea.

2. Exaspération :
- ☐ **a.** I'm fed up with all this!
- ☐ **b.** This is so annoying.
- ☐ **c.** Oh I'm terribly sorry!

3. Joie :
- ☐ **a.** This is really terrible.
- ☐ **b.** That's terrific.
- ☐ **c.** I'm over the moon.

4. Désapprobation :
- ☐ **a.** I don't think this is a good idea.
- ☐ **b.** You're supposed to talk to him.
- ☐ **c.** I'd rather go skating.

5. Souhait :
- ☐ **a.** I wish he had come with us.
- ☐ **b.** I wish he would come with us.
- ☐ **c.** It would be great if he came with us.

6. Détermination :
- ☐ **a.** I'm not going to apologize.
- ☐ **b.** I will not apologize.
- ☐ **c.** I don't have to apologize.

7. Mise en garde :
- ☐ **a.** I'm warning you.
- ☐ **b.** How awful!
- ☐ **c.** Don't you dare!

8. Déception :
- ☐ **a.** What a shame!
- ☐ **b.** What a pity!
- ☐ **c.** You're expected to answer the letter.

S'ENTRAÎNER

2 Identifier les fonctions de communication à partir d'un énoncé

Repérez les mots clés dans les énoncés suivants et donnez au moins trois fonctions de communication à mettre en œuvre.

1. Rod eventually agrees to meet Mrs Barley at her office. Mrs Barley, who is very kind and helpful as usual, tries to see what job would best suit Rod in her company.
2. The ambulance arrives. The paramedics tell Olivia that her brother is in a very critical condition. Olivia's mother is furious because Olivia should have sent for an ambulance at once. Olivia feels terribly guilty.
3. Zara, 17, wants to take Jacob (also 17) out. At first, he refuses, but then he agrees... on certain conditions.
4. When Kate finds out that Maya has given away her secret, she is sad and disappointed. She decides to call her friend to tell her off, but Maya argues she did it for Kate's good.

OBJECTIF BAC

3 Préparer l'écriture d'un dialogue

Reprenez la situation n° 3 de l'exercice précédent : proposez deux phrases correspondant à chaque fonction de communication et à la situation.

SE TESTER

1

1. **Conseil : a et c**
2. **Exaspération : a et b**
3. **Joie : b et c**
4. **Désapprobation : a et c**
5. **Souhait : b et c**
6. **Détermination : a et b**
7. **Mise en garde : a et c**
8. **Déception : a et b**

b. Would you like a cup a tea? (offre)
c. Oh! I'm terribly sorry! (regret)
a. This is really terrible. (désespoir)
b. You're supposed to talk to him. (devoir)
a. I wish he had come with us. (regret)
c. I don't have to apologize. (absence d'obligation)
b. How awful! (désespoir)
c. You're expected to answer the letter. (devoir)

S'ENTRAÎNER

2 Les mots clés sont soulignés.

1. Rod eventually agrees to meet Mrs Barley at her office. Mrs Barley, who is very kind and helpful as usual, tries to see what job would best suit Rod in her company.
Fonctions de communication : likes, dislikes, preference, suggestion, ability, inability.
2. The ambulance arrives. The paramedics tell Olivia that her brother is in a very critical condition. Olivia's mother is furious because Olivia should have sent for an ambulance at once. Olivia feels terribly guilty.
Fonctions de communication : anger / reproach, regret, hope.
3. Zara, 17, wants to take Jacob (also 17) out. At first, he refuses, but then he agrees... on certain conditions.
Fonctions de communication : suggestion, refusal, agreement, condition.
4. When Kate finds out that Maya has given away her secret, she is sad and disappointed. She decides to call her friend to tell her off, but Maya argues she did it for Kate's good.
Fonctions de communication : anger / reproach, sadness, disappointment, purpose.

OBJECTIF BAC

3

Suggestion : Why don't we go out together some time ?
Do you fancy going out with me?
Refusal : I'm really sorry but I can't. I'm too busy at the moment, you see.
Well I can't, I'm afraid. I'm too busy at the moment, you see.
Agreement : Well, I suppose that's okay. I can work this out.
All right. I'll see what I can do.
Condition : I'll go out with you if we go and see a James Bond film.
I'll go out with you as long as we have lunch at a fancy restaurant.

Notez que le niveau de langue est courant puisqu'il s'agit d'une conversation entre deux adolescents.

CHAPITRE

5 Écrire une lettre

Cet exercice est classique mais peut revêtir différents aspects. On peut en effet vous demander de rédiger « des lettres personnelles pour décrire expériences et impressions » (niveau B1) ou « des lettres qui mettent en valeur le sens que vous attribuez personnellement aux événements et aux expériences » (niveau B2).
Comme pour la rédaction d'un dialogue, il faut dans les deux cas très bien connaître le texte support de la compréhension et en tenir compte dans la lettre.

I Les types de lettre

On peut vous demander de rédiger une lettre privée ou une lettre formelle. Au vu du développement des nouvelles technologies, il est également fréquent que l'on vous demande de rédiger un courriel ou de contribuer à un site ou à un blog.

- **Les lettres privées** sont destinées à des amis ou à des parents ou même parfois à son journal intime *(secret diary)*. Selon le rapport entre l'expéditeur et le ou les destinataires, le niveau de langue peut être soutenu, courant ou légèrement familier, mais jamais vulgaire.

- **Les lettres formelles** correspondent à différentes situations : lettre de motivation *(cover letter)*, lettre à la rédaction d'un journal ou d'un magazine, lettre à une administration, demande de renseignements, etc. Dans chacun de ces contextes, le niveau de langue doit être plutôt soutenu.

- **Les courriels et pages Internet** sont des supports un peu différents des deux autres. Si vous rédigez une demande de renseignements par courriel, le niveau de langue sera simplement courant et l'agencement ne sera pas aussi strict que pour une lettre formelle. De même, en règle générale, pour une page de blog.

II La présentation de la lettre

- Dans tous les cas, indiquez l'adresse de l'expéditeur, éventuellement son numéro de téléphone, puis la date, en haut à droite. Pour une lettre formelle, on indiquera en plus les coordonnées du destinataire à gauche.
- Les formules d'introduction et de conclusion sont indispensables pour donner un caractère authentique à la lettre. Elles dépendent du destinataire. Voici les plus fréquentes.

ZOOM

Lettres privées, journal intime

formules d'introduction	formules de conclusion (+ signature)
Dear Harry, Dearest Emily, Dear all, Hello! Hi! Hi Harry! Hi everybody! Dear diary,	Love, / Lots of love, / Much love, Keep well, Take care, Write soon, Hope to hear from you soon, Looking forward to hearing from you / to seeing you, Keep in touch,

Dearest, lots of love et much love sont des formules très affectueuses.

Lettres formelles

formules d'introduction	formules de conclusion (+ signature)
Dear Sir or Madam, Dear Sir(s), Dear Madam, Dear Mr / Mrs / Miss Jones Dear Mr and Mrs Jones	Thank you in advance, Yours sincerely, Yours faithfully, Kindest regards,

Mr, Mrs et Miss sont toujours suivis du nom de famille.

FORMULES DE CONCLUSION POUR LES COURRIELS

We shall be back in touch shortly,
We hope to see you again soon,
All good wishes, / Best wishes, / Best,

III Le contenu de la lettre

- Il est indispensable de très bien connaître le texte de départ et de respecter dans la lettre les caractéristiques de la situation et du personnage qui est censé écrire.
- Il est tout aussi nécessaire de lire attentivement les consignes : elles signalent les éléments du texte qu'il faut exploiter et l'identité du destinataire (on n'écrit pas de la même façon à tout le monde). Si le destinataire est un personnage du texte, respectez ses caractéristiques.
- Vous pouvez souligner les mots importants de l'énoncé et repérer dans le texte les éléments qui leur correspondent et serviront d'ossature à votre lettre. Au brouillon, il est nécessaire de noter les caractéristiques de l'expéditeur et du destinataire et de préparer le **plan de la lettre**.
- Lors de la rédaction, il faut éviter de recopier des passages entiers du texte d'origine.

ATTENTION

- L'expéditeur est censé s'exprimer à partir d'une situation et non répéter un récit.
- Il faut écrire à la 1re personne du singulier.

RÉCAPITULONS

- La lettre qu'on vous demande d'écrire n'est pas toujours du même type. Il faut donc analyser attentivement la **consigne**.
- L'agencement et la présentation sont essentiels pour donner à votre production un **aspect authentique**.
- Pour le **contenu**, il faut tenir compte des données du texte de départ ainsi que des consignes.

Se préparer à l'écriture d'une lettre

LA DÉMARCHE

- Je dois adopter une **présentation** conforme à la nature de la lettre.
- Je dois tenir compte du contenu du **texte d'origine**.
- Je dois employer les **formules d'introduction et de conclusion** attendues.

L'EXEMPLE COMMENTÉ

Le texte ci-dessous est le texte d'origine. Il donne la situation de départ.

Ce passage est extrait de l'autobiographie d'une romancière et poétesse noire. La scène se passe dans le Sud des États-Unis au temps de la ségrégation. La narratrice a trouvé un emploi comme domestique chez une blanche, Mrs Cullinan.

" Miss Glory and I were washing up the lunch dishes when Mrs Cullinan came to the doorway. "Mary?"

Miss Glory asked, "Who?"

[…] "I want Mary to go down to Mrs Randall's and take her some soup. She's not been feeling well for a few days."

Miss Glory's face was a wonder to see. "You mean Margaret, ma'am. Her name's Margaret."

"That's too long. She's Mary from now on. Heat that soup from last night and put it in the china tureen and, Mary, I want you to carry it carefully."

Every person I knew had a hellish horror of being "called out of his name." It was a dangerous practice to call a Negro anything that could be loosely construed as insulting because of the centuries of their having been called niggers, jigs, dinges, blackbirds, crows, boots and spooks.

Miss Glory had a fleeting second of feeling sorry for me. Then as she handed me the hot tureen she said, "Don't mind, don't pay that no mind. Sticks and stones may break your bones, but words… You know, I been working for her for twenty years."

> china tureen: soupière en porcelaine
> loosely construed as: plus ou moins interprété comme
> fleeting: bref
> don't pay that no mind; I been working: langue incorrecte, Miss Glory n'a reçu aucune instruction.

She held the back door open for me. "Twenty years. I wasn't much older than you. My name used to be Hallelujah. That's what Ma named me, but my mistress give me 'Glory', and it stuck. I likes it better too." [...] For a few seconds it was a tossup over whether I would laugh (imagine being named Hallelujah) or cry (imagine letting some white woman rename you for her convenience.) My anger saved me from either outburst. I had to quit the job, but the problem was going to be how to do it.

> give; likes: gave; like
> it was a tossup over whether... or...: j'ai vraiment hésité entre... et...

Maya Angelou, *I Know Why the Caged Bird Sings*, 1969.

Margaret writes to her best friend who is black too. She tells her how she feels about Mrs Cullinan, Miss Glory and her future. (150 words)

POUR VOUS AIDER

- Il s'agit de se mettre dans la peau de la narratrice, Margaret, et d'écrire une lettre à la 1re personne du singulier à sa meilleure amie, noire américaine comme elle.
- Le plan de la lettre est indiqué dans la consigne : Margaret doit parler de ses sentiments à l'égard de sa patronne, de l'autre domestique (Miss Glory) et enfin de son désir de partir.

- **Margaret**, narratrice et personnage principal, est noire américaine. Elle est domestique (*"washing up the lunch dishes"*, l. 1).
- **Miss Glory**, l'autre domestique, est naïve : *"Miss Glory's face was a wonder to see. 'You mean Margaret, ma'am. Her name's Margaret'"*, l. 6-7.
- **Miss Cullinan** est une maîtresse autoritaire : *"I want Mary to go"* (l. 4) *That's too long. She's Mary from now on. [...] and Mary, I want you to carry"*, l. 8-10. Elle a d'autorité changé le nom de Margaret en Mary et les deux domestiques ne sont pas censées s'en plaindre : *"That's too long [...] Heat that soup"* (l. 8-9). Elle est représentative des maîtres blancs qui changent à leur gré les noms de leurs domestiques, ce qui devrait être intolérable pour ces derniers : *"Every person I knew [...] spooks"*, l. 11-16.
- Mais cela ne choque pas vraiment **Miss Glory** : *"Miss Glory had a fleeting second of feeling sorry for me"*, l. 17-18. Miss Glory n'est pas instruite et ne semble pas attacher une grande importance aux mots (*"but words..."*, l. 20).

Elle est plus âgée que Margaret : *"I been working for her for twenty years"* (l. 20) *"I wasn't much older than you",* l. 21-22. Elle appartient à une génération qui ne remet pas en question le racisme des Blancs. Elle n'a jamais envisagé de quitter sa place. Elle est docile et satisfaite de son sort : *"My name used to be [...] I likes it better too",* l. 22-24. En outre, elle est assez cordiale: *"Don't mind [...] open for me",* l. 19-21.

Margaret est très différente de Miss Glory et l'attitude de Mrs Cullinan la met en colère : *"imagine letting some white woman rename you for her convenience"*, l. 26-27. Elle appartient à une nouvelle génération, plus instruite et plus combattive que celle de Miss Glory. C'est cette force qui la rend capable d'humour : elle rit du nom de naissance de Miss Glory : *"imagine being named Hallelujah"*, l. 26. Elle tient à se faire respecter ; c'est pourquoi elle veut quitter son emploi même si cela ne semble pas si simple : *"the problem was going to be how to do it"*, l. 28-29.

Proposition de lettre :

809 Dust Street
Stamps,
Arkansas

Dear Beth,

I started my new job yesterday and things don't look good. Mrs Cullinan has changed my name. Margaret is too long a name you see, so I'm Mary now. The woman I work with in the kitchen has been here for twenty years. Her real name is – believe or not – Hallelujah, but Mrs Cullinan renamed her Glory. Miss Glory does not seem to mind. She is obviously content with her "new" name and her fate. She is a lovely woman and she is very kind to me, but she is one of those Blacks who still take white supremacy for granted. To them, humiliation is a way of life. It is not worth telling her that it should not be so. She would not understand.

I must find a way out of this job. I can't say to my mother that I don't like Mrs Cullinan and want to resign. She would kill me.

What do you think I could do?

Please, write soon.

Love,

Margaret

(174 words)

SE TESTER QUIZ

1 Donner de bonnes et de moins bonnes nouvelles

Cochez les phrases donnant de bonnes nouvelles et proposez une traduction pour chacune.

1. ☐ I'm very well.
2. ☐ Things couldn't be better.
3. ☐ I'm ill with the flu.
4. ☐ I'm doing just fine.
5. ☐ I'm exhausted.
6. ☐ I'm (terribly) worried about...
7. ☐ I'm on top form.
8. ☐ I'm over the moon.
9. ☐ I'm depressed.
10. ☐ I'm not very well.

S'ENTRAÎNER

2 Déterminer le type de lettre et le niveau de langue à employer

Repérez les mots clés dans ces énoncés et donnez le type de lettre ainsi que le niveau de langue correspondant. Rédigez ensuite un plan.

1. As a fan of John Lennon, you are expected to write a letter to be published on an English fan website for the anniversary of his death.

2. You want to get a summer job as a park ranger in the USA. Write a cover letter to Acadia National Park.

3. You are studying for six months in New Zealand. Write an e-mail to your family about your daily life, your feelings and your plans.

4. You are a 70-year-old man or woman who used to be a movie star. Write a letter to your 17-year-old grandson or granddaughter about your career, regrets and hopes.

OBJECTIF BAC

3 Rédiger une lettre

You want to get a summer job as a park ranger in the USA. Write a cover letter to Acadia National Park. (150 words)

Rédigez la lettre sans oublier la présentation, les formules d'introduction et de conclusion.

SE TESTER

1 1. ☒ **I'm very well.** *Je vais très bien.*
2. ☒ **Things couldn't be better.** *Ça va on ne peut mieux.*
3. ☐ I'm ill with the flu. *J'ai la grippe.*
4. ☒ **I'm doing just fine.** *Tout va bien.*
5. ☐ I'm exhausted. *Je suis épuisé(e).*
6. ☐ I'm (terribly) worried about… *Je me fais beaucoup de soucis à propos de…*
7. ☒ **I'm on top form.** *Je suis en pleine forme.*
8. ☒ **I'm over the moon.** *Je nage dans le bonheur.*
9. ☐ I'm depressed. *Je suis déprimé(e).*
10. ☐ I'm not very well. *Je ne vais pas très bien.*

S'ENTRAÎNER

2 Les mots clés sont soulignés.

1. As a fan of John Lennon, you are expected to write a letter to be published on an English fan website for the anniversary of his death.
Type de lettre : contribution à un site Internet sous forme de lettre commémorative adressée aux fans anglais dont vous êtes censé partager la passion.
Niveau de langue : courant mais non familier.

2. You want to get a summer job as a park ranger in the USA. Write a cover letter to Acadia National Park.
Type de lettre : lettre de motivation – donc formelle – pour obtenir un emploi saisonnier dans un parc national américain, en pleine nature.
Niveau de langue : soutenu.

3. You are studying for six months in New Zealand. Write an e-mail to your family about your daily life, your feelings and your plans.
Type de lettre : courriel à sa famille – vraisemblablement aux parents – pour décrire sa vie d'étudiant dans un pays anglophone situé aux antipodes.
Niveau de langue : courant, qui peut parfois être un peu familier.

4. You are a 70-year-old man or woman who used to be a movie star. Write a letter to your 17-year-old grandson or granddaughter about your career, regrets and hopes.
Type de lettre : lettre manuscrite destinée à faire un retour en arrière sur son existence et ses choix.
Niveau de langue : courant, mais parfois soutenu à cause de la solennité du ton.

OBJECTIF BAC

3 Proposition de lettre

Human Resources Director
National Park Service
Acadia, Maine

Camille MARTIN

13th January 2013

Dear Mrs Powell,

I am writing to apply for a position as park ranger at Acadia National Park for the summer of 2013.

I am currently studying English Literature and Civilization at La Sorbonne, the University of Paris, France.

I am very interested in this seasonal position and I believe I am well qualified for it.

First, I am a fluent English speaker as I have completed a year studying abroad in a full immersion environment at Berkeley University. So, I'm confident I could converse with American and British visitors as well as French-speaking tourists, of course.

Second, I have a keen interest in science and nature and I should be able to learn facts about the Park's geography and environment.

Last, I am by nature an outgoing and cheerful person, and I believe I could represent the Park well, and would enjoy the role and responsibility.

Thank you in advance for your consideration.
I look forward to hearing back from you.

Yours sincerely,

Camille Martin

(168 words)

CHAPITRE

6 Traiter un sujet de réflexion

Le sujet de réflexion, ou d'argumentation, s'appuie à des degrés divers sur le ou les textes qui ont servi de support à l'exercice de compréhension. Une bonne compréhension de ce ou ces textes est donc indispensable. Il faut aussi prendre le temps de lire très attentivement le sujet. Attention aux hors-sujets !
Votre note dépendra de la pertinence de votre réponse, de la construction et de la cohérence de votre argumentation, ainsi que de la richesse de la syntaxe et du lexique.

I Comprendre le sujet

Identifiez le type de travail qu'on attend de vous. Dans les consignes, repérez les mots clés qui signalent les pistes à suivre, comme, par exemple, la mise en valeur d'une attitude, d'une réaction, d'un sentiment.

A Les types de sujets

Le sujet peut reposer sur le thème principal du ou des textes de départ ou sur un élément plus ciblé de ce ou ces textes. Il peut également être posé à partir d'un document « tremplin » lié à la thématique du ou des textes support(s) de la compréhension écrite.

Sujets en rapport avec le thème principal du ou des textes

Exemples de sujets :

- les progrès scientifiques : *Has scientific progress gone too far?*
- les marques : *How can we account for the tyranny of brands?*
- la vérité : *Should we tell the truth at all costs? Give examples.*
- l'argent : *Can money always buy happiness?*

Sujets sur un élément plus ciblé du ou des textes (une des idées du ou des textes, le comportement d'un personnage...)

Exemples de sujets :
- *"Up early every morning, home late at night, and in between work, nothing but work." Comment on this way of life.*
- *"Have a little ambition, Buddy. You'll never get anywhere in this world unless you've got ambition." To what extent do you agree with Buddy's mother?*

B L'analyse du sujet

Pour éviter le hors-sujet, lisez attentivement l'énoncé et soulignez les mots clés. Comprenez bien ce qu'on attend de vous. Voici quelques décodages de sujets :

How can we account for the tyranny of brands?

Ici, on vous demande d'**expliquer** *(account for)* un phénomène de société. Il vous faudra évoquer des causes, des conséquences et émettre des hypothèses.
- La puissance de la publicité, la société de consommation dont personne n'est protégé.
- Les rapports entre les jeunes (rapports sociaux, rivalité, mode et conformisme, snobisme).
- Vous donnerez enfin votre sentiment sur cette question.

"Have a little ambition, Buddy. You'll never get anywhere in this world unless you've got ambition." To what extent do you agree with Buddy's mother?

To what extent signifie « dans quelle mesure », « jusqu'à quel point ». Vous devrez par conséquent traiter **deux** points.
- En quoi la mère de Buddy a raison (sans ambition on ne va pas très loin, l'ambition est un « moteur » dans la vie, etc.).
- Les limites de ce point de vue : les autres facteurs qui permettent « d'avancer dans ce monde » (situation économique, chance, relations, personnalité).

II L'introduction

On n'introduit bien que ce qu'on connaît bien : dans un premier temps, jetez simplement les bases de l'introduction sur votre brouillon. Vous la finaliserez quand vous aurez bâti l'ensemble de votre devoir et que vous saurez exactement ce qu'il contient. En revanche, gardez-vous bien de donner votre réponse finale dès l'introduction. Réservez-la pour la conclusion.

- Demandez-vous si la question posée dans le sujet gagne à être explicitée et dans quelle mesure vous pouvez exploiter le texte dans votre introduction. Une courte citation ou une reformulation bien choisie peuvent vous aider à « démarrer ».

- Dans l'introduction, ne recopiez jamais l'énoncé. Évoquez-le avec vos propres mots en le faisant apparaître dans un contexte qui introduit déjà une problématique. Évitez les questions directes suivies de platitudes.

III L'argumentation

- On vous demande avant tout d'être **cohérent** : attention aux contradictions. On vous demande aussi d'être **clair** : mettez en valeur les étapes de votre raisonnement en allant à la ligne, en utilisant des conjonctions de coordination, de subordination et quelques mots de liaison bien choisis (pas trop nombreux et naturels si possible). Soignez la ponctuation. Évitez les points d'exclamation.

- Vous pouvez consacrer la première partie à la défense d'un point de vue **(thèse)**, et la deuxième à l'**antithèse**. Quel que soit le sujet, vous vous appuierez toujours sur des **exemples précis** puisés dans le texte et dans votre culture générale. Une bonne connaissance du monde anglophone peut être précieuse.

- La **conclusion** doit être plus qu'un simple résumé de l'argumentation. Votre réponse à la question posée doit y apparaître clairement, mais elle doit être également accompagnée d'une ouverture sur une question ou un sujet plus vaste.

RÉCAPITULONS

- Le sujet de réflexion ou d'argumentation doit être **analysé avec rigueur** afin d'éviter le hors-sujet.
- Il faut veiller à la **cohérence** de l'argumentation et maîtriser le contenu du développement avant de rédiger l'introduction et la conclusion.
- Il faut s'efforcer d'employer un **niveau de langue soutenu** et des structures variées.

Écrire un texte argumenté

LA DÉMARCHE

- Je dois bien **expliciter les consignes** pour éviter le hors-sujet.
- Je soigne la **construction** de mon argumentation ainsi que l'expression.
- Je rédige une **introduction** et une **conclusion** avec soin.

L'EXEMPLE COMMENTÉ

In Britain there is one CCTV camera for every fourteen people. In your view, are these cameras a blessing or a curse? (300 words)

- Le sujet porte sur les caméras de surveillance. Il s'agit de réfléchir au bien-fondé de la présence de ces caméras.

ph © Steve Forrest / Insight / Panos / REA

- **Texte proposé**

INTRODUCTION

Il faut éviter les phrases du type : Are CCTV cameras a blessing or a curse? This is a burning issue. (Est-ce que les caméras de surveillance sont une bonne ou une mauvaise chose ? Voilà une question brûlante.) Il vaut mieux partir d'une remarque générale et trouver une expression synonyme pour évoquer la question posée.

People my age, whether in Britain or France, have grown with CCTV cameras and few of us complain about them. A lot of older people, who have witnessed the emergence and the multiplication of those cameras, argue that they are a threat to individual freedom. Today, western governments are obsessed with security and in this context the question is whether CCTV cameras do more harm than good.

PREMIÈRE PARTIE

Il faut exposer les raisons qui poussent les autorités à utiliser ce moyen de surveillance : prévention du terrorisme et de la criminalité, volonté de rassurer la population. Il faut ensuite illustrer par des exemples.

CCTV cameras are often said to be useful. They enable the authorities to fight against terrorism and crime. Governments also want to take precautions to prevent criticism in case something nasty happens. On the whole, they want insecure people to feel safer. For example, the perpetrators of the 2005 terrorist attacks in London were soon identified thanks to CCTV cameras. Therefore these tools might well prevent other attacks.

DEUXIÈME PARTIE

Il faut maintenant expliquer pourquoi certaines personnes désapprouvent ce moyen de surveillance : il peut servir à espionner les gens et ainsi limiter leur liberté. Se savoir observé revêt un aspect extrêmement dérangeant.

On the other hand, these cameras can also be seen as a threat to individual freedom. Surveillance is one of those corollaries of scientific progress which makes it more and more easy to spy on people and locate them thanks to credit cards, mobile phones, the Internet, Oyster cards in public transport. Some people feel that someone is constantly keeping an eye on them and even if they have nothing to hide this can be unpleasant. In Britain there is one CCTV camera for every fourteen people. This is often criticised in the British press. CCTV cameras can be viewed as the warning of worse things to come.

CONCLUSION

Il faut répondre à la question soit par l'approbation [a blessing] soit par le rejet [a curse] et élargir le problème.

I do not mind CCTV cameras at all, I am not afraid of them, quite the opposite. I think CCTV cameras are innocuous *(inoffensives)* and that they are indispensable in the dangerous world we live in. Besides, those who claim that their freedom is being threatened should try to understand that there is no freedom if there is no security.

OU :

CCTV cameras make me feel uncomfortable and I think they are utterly useless. Nothing will ever stop the determination of thieves, murderers or terrorists. Moreover, CCTV cameras are not just about safety and freedom. They are also about money. They are costly and the money that is spent on most of them had better be spent on more pressing issues. [301 words]

SE TESTER QUIZ

1 Utiliser les conjonctions de subordination

Cochez la traduction correcte de la conjonction en gras.

1. **Even though** they have talent they cannot make a living out of their hobby.
❑ **a.** De peur que ❑ **b.** Même si

2. **Considering that** people do not feel safe, they will opt for this new policy.
❑ **a.** Étant donné que ❑ **b.** Seulement si

3. More and more young adults tend to live with their parents **since** jobs are scarce.
❑ **a.** puisque ❑ **b.** depuis que

4. Employers wanted them to work overtime **so that** they could earn more money.
❑ **a.** pour que ❑ **b.** si bien que

5. You'll enjoy English a lot more **once** you start enlarging your vocabulary.
❑ **a.** dès que ❑ **b.** une fois que

6. People don't protest **although** they are extremely dissatisfied.
❑ **a.** si bien que ❑ **b.** bien que

7. **As** there are more and more homeless people the authorities should do something.
❑ **a.** Tandis que ❑ **b.** Comme

8. It is **as though** money, success and power are the only values she believes in.
❑ **a.** alors que ❑ **b.** comme si

9. **Unless** these laws are implemented, children will keep on being exploited.
❑ **a.** Si ❑ **b.** À moins que

10. These people suffer **as soon as** they are laid off.
❑ **a.** dès que ❑ **b.** bien que

S'ENTRAÎNER

2 Préparer le plan d'une argumentation

Pour chaque sujet, soulignez les mots clés. Essayez de bien comprendre le sens de la question, définissez les points à traiter et envisagez un plan. Pensez aux champs lexicaux et aux notions que vous pourrez exploiter.

1. Discuss: There are few women at the top and it is their own fault.
2. What are the advantages and drawbacks of home-schooling?

OBJECTIF BAC

3 Écrire un texte argumenté

En vous aidant du document « tremplin », extrait de *The Closed Circle*, traitez le sujet de réflexion suivant :

How do you account for the fact that so many people pay so much attention to TV celebrities, and so little to men and women whose work really matters? (300 words)

Un journaliste anglais, Doug Anderton, espionne un certain Paul dans un restaurant.

"His gaze was fixed [...] on a scene unfolding in the corner of the restaurant nearest to the entrance, where the young couple who had arrived just behind Paul in a white stretch limo were enjoying the attentions of a crowd of journalists and photographers. This couple, whom Paul had not recognized, had last year been two of the contestants on Britain's most popular primetime reality TV show. For weeks they had kept the public guessing as to whether or not they were going to have sex with each other on camera. The tabloid papers had devoted hundreds of column inches to the subject. Neither of them had talent, or wisdom, or education, or even much personality to speak of. But they were young and good-looking, and they dressed well, and they had been on television, and that was enough. And so the photographers kept taking pictures, and the journalists kept trying to make them say something quotable or amusing (which was difficult, because they had no wit, either). Meanwhile, Doug could not help noticing, right next to them, waiting for his wife to emerge from the ladies', the figure of Professor John Copland: Britain's leading geneticist, one of its better-selling science writers, and regularly mentioned as a potential Nobel prizewinner. But no one was taking his photograph, or asking him to say anything. He could have been a cab driver, waiting to drive one of the guests home, as far as anybody else was concerned. And for Doug, this situation encapsulated so perfectly everything he wanted to say about Britain in 2002 – the obscene weightlessness of its cultural life, the grotesque triumph of sheen over substance, all the clichés which were only clichés, as it happened, because they were true – that he was, perversely, pleased to be witnessing it.

Jonathan Coe, *The Closed Circle*, 2004.

contestants: candidats
tabloid papers: presse populaire
wisdom: sagesse
quotable: digne d'être cité
wit: esprit, intelligence
the ladies': les toilettes pour femmes
cab: taxi
encapsulate: incarner
weightlessness: apesanteur (ici, légèreté excessive)
sheen: le clinquant

SE TESTER

1 1. Even though — **b.** Même si
2. Considering that — **a.** Étant donné que
3. since — **a.** puisque
4. so that — **a.** pour que
5. once — **b.** une fois que
6. although — **b.** bien que
7. As — **b.** Comme
8. as though — **b.** comme si
9. Unless — **b.** À moins que
10. as soon as — **a.** dès que

S'ENTRAÎNER

2 Les mots clés sont soulignés.

1. Discuss: There are few women at the top and it is their own fault.
Discuss → Explain the statement and react.
Plan possible:
– Is this statement a mere provocation or is it true that some women do not try their best to reach the top? (What are their excuses?)
– Show that the scarcity *(rareté)* of women at the top is due to many other reasons.
– Give your own views on the issue.
Vocabulary: work, family / motherhood, responsibilities, the workload *(la charge de travail)*, sexism, machismo, the "glass ceiling".
Notions: preventing, inability.

2. What are the advantages and drawbacks of home-schooling?
Advantages and drawbacks → in other words the pros and cons.
Plan possible:
– The advantages.
– The drawbacks.
– Your opinion / conclusion.
Vocabulary: learning, working at your own pace, no commuting, more spare time; loneliness, boredom, a narrow view of life, inability to work in a team; home-schooling in the USA (often on religious grounds).
Notions: purpose, enabling, preventing, consequence.

OBJECTIF BAC

3 Proposition de corrigé

Introduction

Today, a lot of people believe that fame is the best thing that can happen to someone and TV celebrities have become the most important people in the world. It does not occur to most people that scientists, intellectuals and genuine artists might be worthy of more attention. But this is hardly surprising.

Argumentation

• Première partie

TV celebrities get lots of attention because they are "accessible", and not just because there is a TV in every household.
First, after a hard day at work, watching prime time TV is easy. You are not expected to think.
Besides, the dangerous thing about TV celebrities is that they are "perfect". They make you dream. This is childish behaviour, but some viewers enjoy that kind of break from reality.
The status of TV celebrities is evidence that our society is dictated by fame, appearances and money. The media can be blamed for this, but those who worship TV celebrities are their partners in crime. They are happy to live in a hypnotizing world in which all that glitters is gold.

• Deuxième partie

On the other hand, lack of interest in people like Professor John Copland stems from the fact that they are less accessible. Only a limited, educated audience can understand them, and complex explanations about genetics require concentration and effort.
Also, geniuses often live a secluded life. Few people know what they look like and you cannot identify with someone you have never seen.
Being "invisible", not particularly rich and not always good-looking, geniuses are unlikely to make the average person dream, no matter how useful their work is.

Conclusion

TV celebrities have become the new opium of the people. Our society worships the wrong people, however I doubt Professor John Copland and his colleagues wish they were stalked by fans or paparazzi. (297 words)

CHAPITRE

7 Prononcer correctement

Le Cadre européen commun de référence pour les langues (CECRL) accorde une grande importance à l'expression orale et donc à la qualité de la prononciation. C'est pourquoi elle est évaluée au baccalauréat quelle que soit la série.

Pour vous entraîner à l'oral, retrouvez les zones de texte marquées sur le site www.prepabac.com/media.

I La transcription phonétique

La phonétique pour quoi faire ? Quand vous cherchez un mot anglais dans le dictionnaire, vous devez en apprendre l'orthographe (pour l'écrire) et la prononciation (pour le dire), d'où la nécessité de savoir lire la transcription phonétique. Une bonne maîtrise de la phonétique vous permet aussi de noter la prononciation des mots au fur et à mesure que vous les apprenez, que ce soit en cours ou à d'autres moments.

A Les voyelles

voyelles brèves		voyelles réduites (car non accentuées)		voyelles longues	
fit	/ɪ/	awake, America	/ə/	dream, feed	/iː/
pen	/e/	event (devant consonne)	/ɪ/	food	/uː/
fat	/æ/	wonderful	/ʊ/	bar	/ɑː/
dog	/ɒ/			pork, law	/ɔː/
bus	/ʌ/			burn, learn, bird	/ɜː/
good	/ʊ/				

ATTENTION !
Ne confondez pas /ɪ/ et /iː/ :
shit /ɪ/ ≠ a sheet /iː/ (une feuille de papier) ; a bitch /ɪ/ ≠ a beach /iː/ (une plage)

B Les diphtongues

fight, write	/aɪ/	toy	/ɔɪ/	boat	/əʊ/	fair	/eə/
plate, gay	/eɪ/	house	/aʊ/	beer, dear	/ɪə/	poor	/ʊə/

C Les consonnes

big	/b/	pig	/p/	light	/l/	sleep	/s/
door	/d/	true	/t/	young	/j/	nose	/z/
fun	/f/	cow	/k/	vase	/v/	think	/θ/
grass	/g/	shine	/ʃ/	darling	/ŋ/	this	/ð/
happy	/h/	war	/w/	mum	/m/	match	/tʃ/
pleasure	/ʒ/	run	/r/	no	/n/	age	/dʒ/

ZOOM

Maîtriser les sons difficiles

Écoutez les exemples qui suivent sur le site **www.prepabac.com/media**.

- **Le son** /ə/. C'est le son inaccentué par excellence. Il correspond à plusieurs graphies.

actor particular stronger tomorrow support thorough famous

- **Le son** /ɪ/. Ce son se rapprocherait plutôt du « é » français. Il correspond aussi à plusieurs graphies.

big build image private

- **Le son** /ʌ/. Ce son se rapprocherait plutôt du « a » français.

luck sun dull much

▸ Le son /tʃ/. Très souvent, les francophones ne le prononcent pas de façon assez « dynamique » : ils n'insistent pas assez sur le /t/.

cheat choose watching match

▸ Le son /h/. Le *h* initial est prononcé **sauf** dans **hour, honest** (et ses dérivés), **honour** (et ses dérivés) et **heir(ess)** (héritier, ère). En revanche, il ne faut pas prononcer de *h* là où il n'y en a pas. Cela peut aboutir à des confusions embarrassantes. Par exemple, si l'on dit harm /hɑːm/ (du mal) au lieu de arm /ɑːm/ (bras).

▸ Les sons /θ/ et /ð/ (qui correspondent à *th*). Ils ne se prononcent ni /s/ ni /z/. Ces confusions peuvent entraîner des malentendus.

/θ/ ne se prononce pas /s/ (thing ≠ sing) et /ð/ ne se prononce pas /z/ (then ≠ zen).

II Prononcer les mots correctement

A Accentuer les syllabes accentuées (pas les autres)

Écoutez les exemples qui suivent sur le site **www.prepabac.com/media**.

Dans les dictionnaires, la syllabe accentuée est précédée du signe ˈ : /æmˈbɪʃn/. Elle peut aussi être signalée en gras : /æm**bɪʃ**n/.

Exemples de mots accentués sur une seule syllabe

agree /əˈgriː/ agreement /əˈgriːmənt/ govern /ˈgʌvn/ government /ˈgʌvnmənt/

Exemples de mots avec accent primaire / principal (la syllabe portant cet accent se fera davantage entendre) **et accent secondaire** (la syllabe portant cet accent se fera plus entendre que le reste, mais moins que la syllabe portant l'accent principal).

consolation /ˌkɒnsəˈleɪʃn/ mathematics /ˌmæθəˈmætɪks/

B Respecter les voyelles réduites (= non accentuées)

Écoutez les exemples qui suivent sur le site **www.prepabac.com/media**.

On entend à peine la dernière voyelle dans les mots qui se terminent en :

- **consonne + *le*** : respectable /rɪˈspektəbl/, miracle /ˈmɪrəkl/, simple /ˈsɪmpl/
- **voyelle + *l*** : animal /ˈænɪml/, towel /ˈtaʊəl/

- Les suffixes *-ion, -ial, -ious, -ity, -ic, -ics* déterminent la place de l'accent de mot : la syllabe qui les précède est accentuée.

imagine /ɪ'mædʒɪn/	→	imagination /ɪˌmædʒɪ'neɪʃn/
industry /'ɪndəstri/	→	industrial /ɪn'dʌstriəl/, industrious /ɪn'dʌstriəs/
sensitive /'sensətɪv/	→	sensitivity /ˌsensə'tɪvəti/
history /'hɪstri/	→	historic /hɪs'tɒrɪk/
gymnast /'dʒɪmnæst/	→	gymnastics /dʒɪm'næstɪks/

ATTENTION
Catholic, Arabic (la langue arabe), a lunatic (un fou) et politics (la politique) sont accentués sur la première syllabe.

S'ENTRAÎNER AVEC QUELQUES MOTS SOUVENT MAL PRONONCÉS

enough /ɪ'nʌf/	study /'stʌdi/, student /'stjuːdnt/
author /'ɔːθə/	title /'taɪtl/
published /'pʌblɪʃt/	interesting /'ɪntrɪstɪŋ/
now /naʊ/	determined /dɪ'tɜːmɪnd/
about /ə'baʊt/	don't /dəʊnt/
half /hɑːf/	child /tʃaɪld/, children /'tʃɪldrən/
young /jʌŋ/	write /raɪt/, wrote /rəʊt/, written /'rɪtn/, a writer /'raɪtə/

III Prononcer les phrases correctement

Écoutez les exemples qui suivent sur le site **www.prepabac.com/media**.

A Les mots les plus accentués

- Les mots lexicaux sont d'autant plus accentués qu'ils apportent une information importante.

I **forgot** to **tell** you! I met **Bob** yesterday. Bob is a **funny guy**, you **know**.

Le premier *Bob* est plus accentué que le second : c'est la première fois qu'il apparaît dans la conversation où il apporte quelque chose de nouveau.

- Comparez : Anna saw a **rat** in the garage et Anna saw a rat in the **garage**.
Dans la première phrase, l'information essentielle est qu'il y a un rat (et non pas une grenouille) : *rat* porte l'accent principal. Dans la seconde phrase, l'information essentielle est l'endroit où se trouve la bête : *garage* porte l'accent principal.

- **En règle générale, les mots grammaticaux ne sont pas accentués.**

  Tim wasn't **sure** he **wanted** to **go** to the **park**.
  /'tɪm wɒznt 'ʃʊə hi 'wɒntɪd tə 'gəʊ tə ðə 'pɑːk/

sauf :

- en fin de phrase ;

  What are you talking **about**?

- pour exprimer une emphase ou un contraste.

  "**Who** broke my cup?" (who: mot clé = accentué)
  "Eva."
  "I didn't! **You** did!" (Ce n'est pas moi, c'est toi !)

B L'intonation

Intonation montante ↗

- *Yes / No questions* — Is he French? ↗
- Ton sympathique, joyeux, fier — I'm so happy to see you again!! ↗
- Mises en garde aimables — Mind the step. ↗
- Invitations — Follow me. ↗

Intonation descendante ↘

- Questions en *wh-* et *how* — What are you doing here? ↘ How old are you? ↘
- Ton neutre ou triste — We have no idea where she is. ↘
- Ordre (neutre ou autoritaire) — Follow me. ↘

RÉCAPITULONS

- La prononciation doit être **la plus authentique possible** si l'on veut se faire comprendre de son interlocuteur.
- Il faut connaître les règles qui régissent **l'accent de mot** et **l'accent de phrase**.
- **L'intonation** est également très importante. Une intonation fautive peut vous rendre incompréhensible ou donner un autre sens à votre message.

Prononcer les sons difficiles

LA DÉMARCHE

- Je me familiarise avec **l'alphabet phonétique**.
- Je m'entraîne à **prononcer** les sons difficiles.
- Je pense à adopter la bonne **intonation**, c'est-à-dire à accentuer correctement les mots et les phrases.

L'EXEMPLE COMMENTÉ

Écoutez les exemples qui suivent sur le site **www.prepabac.com/media**.

- Malgré des ressemblances orthographiques, ces mots **ne se prononcent pas de la même façon**. Écoutez-les et répétez-les.

enough through though laugh caught draught

- Attention ! La règle française disant que le **« s » entre deux voyelles** se prononce /z/ et non /s/ ne s'applique pas en anglais ! Inversement, deux « s » peuvent se prononcer /z/. Écoutez et comparez.

disobey based increase rise possess obsessed

- Les mots suivants sont des **paires minimales** : un seul son diffère d'un mot à l'autre. Écoutez-les et répétez-les.

big / bug dill / dull bid / bud harm / arm
shore / chore thick / sick they / say fit / feet

- Écoutez ces ***tongue-twisters*** (« tordeurs de langue ») et essayez de les répéter le plus vite possible.

Red lorry, yellow lorry.
Black background, brown background.
Six sleek swans swam swiftly southwards.
Elizabeth's birthday is on the first Thursday of this month.
Five fuzzy French frogs frolicked through the fields in France.
Round and round the rugged rocks the ragged rascals ran.

lorry: camion • background: arrière-plan • sleek swans: cygnes aux plumes lisses et brillantes • southwards: vers le sud • fuzzy: confuses • frolic: gambader • rugged rocks: rochers déchiquetés • ragged rascals: voyous en guenilles

Tous ces exercices sont enregistrés sur le site www.prepabac.com/media.

SE TESTER QUIZ

1 Prononcer des sons difficiles

Cochez le mot qui contient le son indiqué. Répétez les mots puis traduisez-les.

1. /θ/ ☐ **a.** truth ☐ **b.** truce
2. /ð/ ☐ **a.** also ☐ **b.** although
3. /tʃ/ ☐ **a.** shoes ☐ **b.** choose
4. /ɪ/ ☐ **a.** live ☐ **b.** leave
5. /ə/ ☐ **a.** author ☐ **b.** orange
6. /ə/ ☐ **a.** bar ☐ **b.** cellular

S'ENTRAÎNER

2 Retrouver les mots à partir de leur transcription phonétique

Lisez ces mots, écrivez-les puis entraînez-vous à les répéter.

1. /ˈrɪznəbl/
2. /ˈfɪnɪʃt/
3. /faɪn/
4. /ˈdefnəs/
5. /ˈgreɪʃəs/
6. /əˈmeɪzɪŋ/
7. /ˈfeəli/
8. /ˌɪnkrəˈdjuːləti/
9. /kləʊðz/

3 Attention aux suffixes

Soulignez la syllabe accentuée puis vérifiez à l'écoute et répétez les mots.

1. disability
2. determination
3. Atlantic
4. lunatic
5. mysterious
6. fabulous
7. material
8. phenomenal
9. motherhood

OBJECTIF BAC

4 Identifier les mots accentués et l'intonation

Soulignez les mots accentués, puis indiquez par des flèches l'intonation des phrases : montante ↗ ou descendante ↘.

"Come quick, Grandma! There's a leak in the bathroom. The floor is covered in water!"

"WHAT, LILY? A FREAK IN THE BATHROOM? WHO IS HE?"

"Not a freak, Grandma. A leak! Water! Do you hear me?"

leak /liːk/: fuite
freak /friːk/: type bizarre

SE TESTER

1 1. /θ/ a. **truth** *(vérité)* b. truce *(trêve)*
2. /ð/ a. also *(également)* b. **although** *(bien que)*
3. /tʃ/ a. shoes *(chaussures)* b. **choose** *(choisir)*
4. /ɪ/ a. **live** *(vivre)* b. leave *(quitter, partir)*
5. /ə/ a. **author** *(auteur)* b. orange
6. /ə/ a. bar *(bar)* b. **cellular** *(cellulaire)*

S'ENTRAÎNER

2 1. reasonable 2. finished 3. fine 4. deafness 5. gracious 6. amazing 7. fairly 8. incredulity 9. clothes

3 1. disa**bi**lity *ity* = suffixe fort : détermine la place de l'accent de mot
2. determi**na**tion *ion* = suffixe fort
3. At**lan**tic *ic* = suffixe fort
4. **lu**natic exception à la règle des mots en *-ic*
5. mys**te**rious *ious* = suffixe fort
6. **fa**bulous *ous* = suffixe faible : ne détermine pas la place de l'accent
7. ma**te**rial *ial* = suffixe fort
8. phe**no**menal *al* = suffixe faible, comme *ous*
9. **mo**therhood *hood* = suffixe faible, comme *ous, al*

OBJECTIF BAC

4 "**Come quick, Grandma**! ↘ There's a **leak** in the **bathroom**. ↘ The **floor** is **covered** in water!" ↘
"**What, Lily**? ↘ A **freak** in the **bathroom**? ↗ **Who** is he?" ↘
"Not a **freak**, **Grandma**. ↘ A **leak**! ↘ **Water**! ↘ Do you **hear** me?" ↗

Le deuxième freak est particulièrement accentué : Lily corrige sa grand-mère (emphase).

CHAPITRE

8 Comprendre un document sonore

Vous vous exercez régulièrement en cours de langue à la compréhension orale. Cette compétence est évaluée au baccalauréat dans toutes les séries, sauf L. Après trois écoutes séparées par une pause d'une minute à chaque fois, vous devrez restituer en français un document sonore ou vidéo de 90 secondes maximum (monologue ou dialogue). Pendant l'année de 1re, il est avant tout nécessaire de vous entraîner aux techniques mises en œuvre lors d'un exercice de compréhension orale.

I Conseils généraux

- Comme la compréhension écrite, la compréhension orale repose sur deux phases essentielles : le recueil d'indices et leur traitement. L'absence de support écrit est souvent considérée comme une difficulté supplémentaire. Cependant, comme vous le faites pour la compréhension de l'écrit, vous pouvez vous aider des **éléments identifiés** pour comprendre au moins les idées principales du texte enregistré et pour tenter de reconstruire le **message**.

- L'oreille peut et doit être entraînée ; pour cela, il y a bien entendu vos cours. Mais saisissez aussi toutes les occasions d'améliorer votre compréhension de l'oral.

– Regardez des films en **V. O., sous-titrée en anglais** : cet exercice vous permet d'associer prononciation et orthographe.

– Allez sur les **sites anglophones** britanniques (notamment deux sites de la BBC : bbc.co.uk/radio/ et bbclearningenglish.com) et américains (learningenglish.voanews.com et npr.org). Ils vous permettent d'écouter de courts sujets d'actualité que vous pouvez télécharger avec leur script.

- Maîtrisez la **transcription phonétique** (→ p. 74-75). Elle vous aide à mieux reconnaître ce que vous entendez. Prenez l'habitude, lorsque vous consultez le dictionnaire, de vérifier la transcription phonétique des mots (elle apparaît entre crochets ou entre barres obliques) et, lorsque vous apprenez un mot nouveau, d'en noter la transcription phonétique.

II Méthodologie de l'écoute

Il n'est pas nécessaire de comprendre chaque mot du document audio. La progression de la compréhension s'articule autour des étapes suivantes.

A Anticiper

Il s'agit d'émettre des hypothèses pour cerner le sujet en vous appuyant sur le titre du reportage ou de l'interview par exemple. Celui-ci est **systématiquement** donné. Cela va déjà **orienter votre écoute** : en effet, vos attentes ne seront pas les mêmes selon que vous allez écouter un enregistrement intitulé *The Real James Bond* ou *Stopping Malaria with Mobile Phones*.

B Repérer

- Soyez attentifs aux **bruits de fond** ou aux bruits extérieurs : ils peuvent parfois vous fournir des indices.
- Ne paniquez pas dès qu'un mot vous a échappé : vous pourrez sans doute reconstruire le sens du message à partir de ce que vous avez compris.
- Au fil des trois écoutes, repérez **tous les mots accentués**. Ce sont les mots qui portent le message : ce sont principalement les noms, adjectifs, adverbes et verbes lexicaux (→ p. 77-78). Les **mots connus** (et vous en connaissez un certain nombre) « émergent » d'emblée pour vous.
- Soyez efficace dans la **prise de notes**, qui doit être **organisée** dès la première écoute.
- Au fur et à mesure des écoutes et surtout pendant la minute qui sépare chaque écoute, vous émettrez des hypothèses. Vous serez ainsi capable de relier ces mots pour **construire le sens du message**.

• 1re écoute : repérez les éléments clés

Organisez vos notes sous forme de tableau en regroupant, par exemple, les éléments sous différentes catégories : intervenants, dates, lieux, faits... Cette classification des éléments perçus doit faciliter leur mise en relation.

- **Nombre d'intervenants**, leur sexe, fonction, titre, nom, accent...
- **Repères temporels** : dates, indices d'une chronologie *(now, today, then, at that time, in 1952...)*
- **Indications de lieux** : *London, New York, the Bank of England, the White House , the City...*
- **Temps** : présent simple, *present perfect*, prétérit (→ chapitre 18) ; ce sont des indices précieux permettant de déduire si l'on parle de vérités générales, d'actions ou d'états révolus ou toujours en cours, de référence à l'avenir, d'hypothèse...

Recherchez une logique dans l'enchaînement de ces éléments. Imaginons que dans un document les éléments suivants apparaissent : *pub / London / national heritage / homely atmosphere / wood in the décor / open fire / 14th century*... Il n'est pas difficile d'en déduire que l'on vous parle d'un pub (ou de pubs) à Londres, de leur histoire *(14th century)*, de leur aspect *(wood in the décor / open fire)* et de leur ambiance *(homely atmosphere)*.

• 2e écoute : affinez les informations

– Complétez par les **détails** concernant les dates, les chiffres, les statistiques.

– Analysez le ton du locuteur et les **variations d'intonation** : il vous permettront d'aller plus loin dans la compréhension de l'enregistrement.

– L'anglais est une **langue accentuelle**, certains mots « émergent » davantage que d'autres quand vous écoutez une phrase. Les mots importants sont toujours fortement accentués et l'accentuation peut varier selon le terme et le sens que le locuteur cherche à donner à sa phrase.

> Jane! How **could** you do this to me?
> Jane ! Mais comment as-tu bien pu me faire ça ?
>
> Jane! How could **you** do this to me?
> Jane ! Comment toi, tu as pu me faire ça ?
>
> Jane! How could you do **this** to me?
> Jane ! Comment as-tu pu me faire une chose pareille ?

– **L'intonation** de la phrase nous informe sur le sens de celle-ci (→ p. 78).

• 3e écoute : vérifiez vos hypothèses

Relisez vos notes tout en écoutant le document pour confirmer ce que vous avez écrit et faire éventuellement des ajouts. Il s'agit de construire du sens à partir de ce que vous avez compris.

RÉCAPITULONS

Au niveau de la 1re, il faut acquérir les techniques de **repérage** et d'**organisation** de l'information avant tout.

Restituer un document sonore

LA DÉMARCHE

- J'anticipe le contenu du document à l'aide du **titre**.
- Je repère et note les **mots accentués** pendant et entre chacune des trois écoutes.
- Je prête également attention à l'**intonation.**
- Je rédige un **compte rendu** en français.

L'EXEMPLE COMMENTÉ

Pour vous entraîner à l'oral, retrouvez ce document sur le site www. prepabac.com/media.

Allen: environmental disaster

- **Avant l'écoute**, on sait qu'il s'agit d'un monologue et les mots transparents du titre (*disaster* : désastre, catastrophe) nous renseignent sur le thème du document : il s'agit de la pollution environnementale.

- **Pendant les trois écoutes et dans les intervalles**, les informations clés (en majorité des mots accentués) sont relevées puis classées. Les mots en gras sont les mots sur lesquels le locuteur a voulu particulièrement insister et qui permettront une compréhension fine du contenu.

- **1re écoute**

Tout d'abord, il est important de remarquer que l'on entend un bruit de fond, qui ressemble à celui de voitures.

Intervenant	Allen (accent américain)
Repères temporels	*the most recent one (catastrophe) – a year and a half ago – to prevent this stuff for the future – we're going to put in new rules and regulations*
Indications de lieux	*American spectrum – Gulf of Mexico*
Temps	*Past tenses, present simple* *It's not BP who caused the oil spill – **we** caused that catastrophe – there's SUVs* (4 x 4) *and dependence on oil – we vote with our behavior – our behavior **does not** suggest that we want to **change anything** in terms of the environment*

Faits	*you also asked about environmental catastrophe – BP oil spill*

2e écoute

Quelques points peuvent être affinés.

- Les conséquences de la catastrophe à l'époque et aujourd'hui *(that was a big deal – they fixed it – nobody even thinks about it anymore – nobody has changed their behavior / how they drive).*
- La cause profonde du problème selon Allen *(the point is... if there were no demand for oil in the first place, we wouldn't have to even bother).*

3e écoute

- Tout en vérifiant ses hypothèses, on peut aussi se concentrer sur le ton de l'intervenant pour essayer de dégager l'implicite.
- Les mots particulièrement accentués *(**we** caused – **does not** suggest that we want to **change anything** in terms of the environment)* nous permettent de conclure qu'Allen est très critique et désabusé à l'égard du manque de mobilisation de ses concitoyens pour préserver l'environnement.
- Il est question d'un événement récent mais l'avenir est également envisagé.
- Pour parler de l'accident, Allen utilise les temps du passé mais il emploie aussi le présent (présent simple et *present perfect*) pour tirer des conclusions sur l'attitude des Américains confrontés à ce genre de catastrophe.

Exemple de compte rendu

L'intervenant, Allen, donne son opinion sur la pollution environnementale aux États-Unis. Il cite d'abord l'exemple de la catastrophe la plus récente au moment de l'entretien, à savoir la marée noire provoquée par le groupe BP dans le Golfe du Mexique. Mais selon lui, tout est à présent oublié puisque la fuite a été réparée, et cette catastrophe n'a pas modifié le comportement des Américains : ils continuent à rouler en 4 x 4 et à être dépendants du pétrole. Ils sont donc responsables car ils ne sont pas prêts à changer leur mode de vie pour empêcher une telle catastrophe de se reproduire. Les nouvelles lois sur l'environnement ne servent à rien ; ce qu'il faut c'est cesser de dépendre du pétrole.

Écoutez l'enregistrement *Sarah talks about the Royal Family* trois fois en respectant entre chaque écoute une pause d'une minute.

SE TESTER QUIZ

1 Repérer les mots accentués

Cochez les mots que vous avez entendus et, si vous le pouvez, ajoutez-en d'autres.

☐ rejoined	☐ rejoiced	☐ dressed up	☐ messed up
☐ hits	☐ hats	☐ air	☐ hair
☐ press	☐ rest	☐ shame	☐ pain
☐ crude	☐ rude	☐ fortress	☐ faultless
☐ work	☐ walk	☐ bickering	☐ mimicking
☐ dear	☐ clear	☐ world	☐ war

S'ENTRAÎNER

2 Relever les questions dans un dialogue

Complétez les questions entendues avec le mot qui convient.

1. Are you … of the Royal Family?
2. Did you … William and Kate's wedding or more recently the Queen's Jubilee?
3. Do you agree with the people who claim that … is "an idea whose time has passed"?
4. Prince Harry is not really a … to the Royal Family. What's your view on him?
5. Queen Victoria reigned for nearly 64 years and is considered a kind of icon. Do you think Elizabeth II will reach the same … ?
6. Who do you think should become the … to the throne after Queen Elizabeth's reign?

OBJECTIF BAC

3 Écrire un compte rendu en français

Faites maintenant le compte rendu en français de ce document. Pensez à bien relier les mots accentués entre eux.

SE TESTER

1 rejoiced - dressed up - hats - air - press - shame - crude - faultless - work - mimicking - clear - world

S'ENTRAÎNER

2 **1.** Are you **fond** of the Royal Family?
2. Did you **watch** William and Kate's wedding or more recently the Queen's Jubilee?
3. Do you agree with the people who claim that **monarchy** is "an idea whose time has passed"?
4. Prince Harry is not really a **credit** to the Royal Family. What's your view on him?
5. Do you think Elizabeth II will reach the same **status**?
6. Who do you think should become the **heir** to the throne after Queen Elizabeth's reign?

OBJECTIF BAC

3 **Proposition de corrigé**

Sarah, qui est britannique, explique qu'elle a de l'affection pour la famille royale d'Angleterre. Par exemple, elle a été très affectée par la mort de Diana. En outre, elle a suivi le mariage de Kate et William avec enthousiasme. Voir la retransmission de l'événement à la télévision avec toutes ces personnes célèbres, certaines parfois bizarrement habillées, lui a beaucoup plu. Grâce au couple princier, la monarchie garde toute sa popularité et sa raison d'être.
Cependant, le Prince Harry n'est pas aussi populaire en raison de son comportement souvent grossier et de mauvais goût. Par exemple, il s'est un jour déguisé en officier nazi pour se rendre à un bal costumé. Cela dit, certains jeunes le défendent et aiment son côté décontracté.
Enfin, elle ne pense pas qu'Elizabeth II atteindra jamais le statut « d'icône », comme ce fut le cas pour Victoria, mais espère que Kate et William donneront un nouveau visage à la monarchie.

CHAPITRE

9 S'exprimer à l'oral en continu

Cet exercice constitue la première partie de l'épreuve d'expression orale au baccalauréat. Il consiste en une présentation d'une des quatre notions au programme du cycle terminal : **mythes et héros, espaces et échanges, lieux et formes du pouvoir et l'idée de progrès.**

I Description de l'épreuve

A Les différentes filières

- Tous les élèves de toutes les séries doivent passer une épreuve d'expression orale, même si celle-ci peut varier d'une filière à l'autre.
- **Pour les séries ES, S et technologiques**, la notion à présenter est tirée au sort. **Pour la série L**, l'élève doit présenter des dossiers et c'est l'examinateur qui choisit la notion.

B Les attentes au niveau 1re

- L'année de 1re est celle de l'entrée dans le cycle terminal. C'est pour cela qu'il faut se préparer dès à présent à l'épreuve de prise de parole en continu, sans pour autant être dans l'urgence de l'examen. Il n'y a pas de temps à perdre mais vous allez pouvoir **engranger tranquillement** mais sûrement des connaissances et savoir-faire que vous pourrez réinvestir durant l'année de Terminale. Rien ne vous empêche, par exemple, de parler lors de l'examen d'un document que vous aurez étudié en classe de 1re.
- Il faut également s'entraîner dès cette année à la **prise de notes** : le temps de préparation de ces épreuves étant souvent très court (5 ou 10 minutes), vous n'aurez jamais le temps de rédiger entièrement.

II Se familiariser avec les notions

- Dès l'année de 1re, constituez quatre dossiers différents : un par notion. Les traductions varient souvent selon les manuels : choisissez celles que votre professeur utilise.

Voici des suggestions : ***Myths and Heroes*** **(Mythes et héros),** ***Space and Exchanges*** **(Espaces et échanges),** ***Seats and Forms of Power*** **(Lieux et formes du pouvoir) et** ***The Notion of Progress*** **(L'idée de progrès).** Tout au long de l'année, vous y classerez les supports étudiés en cours en explicitant leur lien avec la notion à l'aide d'une problématique.

- Il faut aussi dès maintenant vous familiariser avec le lexique que vous utiliserez pour parler de chaque notion. Pour chacune d'entre elles, nous vous proposons ci-dessous deux angles d'attaque, mais il en existe bien d'autres.

ZOOM

Thématiques et lexique liés aux notions

▸ Mythes et héros

Exemple 1 : Dans quelle mesure les héros ont-ils un impact sur notre vie quotidienne ?

Exemple 2 : Un héros monstrueux peut-il être fascinant ?

a hero / an antihero
a role model : un modèle
a famous / mythical / legendary figure
a supernatural being : un être surnaturel
a real ≠ imaginary character
influence = have an impact on

set an example : donner l'exemple
achieve / accomplish great things: accomplir de grandes choses
emulate sb : imiter qqn
look up to sb : admirer qqn

Espaces et échanges

Exemple 1 : Peut-on encore croire au « Rêve américain » ?

Exemple 2 : Notre planète est-elle vraiment devenue un « village mondial » ?

go / travel abroad : aller / voyager à l'étranger
a foreign country : un pays étranger
a foreigner : un étranger
a stranger : un inconnu
get to know sb : faire la connaissance de qqn
similarities and differences
globalisation : la mondialisation

Lieux et formes du pouvoir

Exemple 1 : L'artiste contestataire a t-il un impact sur le pouvoir en place ?

Exemple 2 : Quel est le pouvoir des médias dans les sociétés occidentales ?

a leader : un dirigeant
the authorities
law and order : la loi et l'ordre
rules = regulations : règles, règlement
protest against : protester contre
a conflict
the media : les médias
privacy : l'intimité, la vie privée
inequality
stand up for equal rights / opportunities : défendre l'égalité des droits / des chances
the balance of power
a counter power
the gender gap : les inégalités entre hommes et femmes
be discriminated against : être victime de discrimination
be prejudiced against sb : avoir des préjugés contre qqn
a scapegoat : un bouc émissaire
a witch hunt : une chasse aux sorcières

L'idée de progrès

Exemple 1 : Les avancées technologiques n'ont-elles que des effets positifs ?

Exemple 2 : Peut-on dire que la place des femmes dans la société évolue vers une plus grande égalité des droits ?

new technologies
progress : le progrès
an advance : un progrès, une avancée
a breakthrough : une découverte, une avancée décisive
evolve : évoluer
improve, get better : s'améliorer
enable sb to do sth : permettre à qqn de faire qqch.
cloning : le clonage
advantages and drawbacks : les avantages et inconvénients
the downside of... : l'inconvénient de...

III S'entraîner à la prise de parole en continu

Durant l'année, vous vous exercerez à la prise de parole en continu, exercice qui ne s'improvise pas. Il s'agit d'un acte de communication dont le sérieux ne doit pas vous échapper sans pour autant vous faire paniquer car il comporte un grand avantage : il vous permet de vous exprimer sans être interrompu ! Il y a cependant deux écueils à éviter : la récitation du cours appris par cœur et, à l'inverse, des hésitations trop nombreuses du fait que vous n'avez probablement pas les documents étudiés sous les yeux lors de l'examen.

A À la maison

- Hors de la classe, vous pouvez vous entraîner chez vous, devant un miroir. Vous pouvez par exemple parler d'un sujet qui vous tient à cœur pendant quelques minutes, en vous efforçant d'avoir un débit le plus fluide possible, même si c'est au détriment de la correction grammaticale.
- De même, prenez l'habitude de restituer de mémoire pendant une ou deux minutes soit les éléments principaux d'un document visuel de votre choix (étudié en classe ou non), soit le plan d'un texte. En étant régulier dans ces différents entraînements qui ont lieu sans la pression du groupe-classe, vous gagnerez rapidement en aisance dans la prise de parole en continu.

B En classe

Pour ce qui est des exercices en classe, outre les règles de prononciation et de grammaire qu'il faudra tenter de respecter à tout moment, voici quelques conseils de conduite à tenir lors de tous vos entraînements.

- **Adoptez une attitude calme et courtoise.** Après vous être assis, prenez soin de poser votre montre sur la table car cela vous permettra de chronométrer discrètement votre prestation. Accordez-vous un instant en mettant vos mains sur la table : cela peut vous aider à vous concentrer.
- **Parlez distinctement** en ayant soin de regarder votre interlocuteur. N'oubliez pas que dans la grande majorité des cas, vous rencontrerez une écoute favorable.
- **Sachez vous abstraire de vos notes** qui doivent d'ailleurs être limitées au plan et aux intitulés des documents évoqués.
- **Choisissez un anglais de qualité.** Veillez à employer un lexique varié et enrichi d'adjectifs et d'adverbes ainsi que de structures grammaticales correctes. Même si votre expression doit être spontanée, il ne s'agit pas de parler comme dans les séries américaines ou les chansons !

N'hésitez pas à vous corriger si vous jugez qu'une expression est maladroite ou si vous avez commis une faute de grammaire. De même, vous pouvez avoir recours aux *gap fillers* (par exemple *well..., actually..., but um..., what I mean is...*) pour vous donner le temps de réfléchir. Mais n'en abusez pas : un bref silence peut vous aider à retrouver le fil de votre démonstration.

IV Présenter une notion

L'évaluation porte sur votre capacité à construire un exposé structuré qui montre que vous avez réfléchi à une problématique et que vous avez dessus un point de vue personnel. Il ne s'agit pas de réciter un cours par cœur.
La démarche à adopter est la suivante :

- **Introduisez et présentez la notion en fonction de l'angle d'attaque** que votre professeur aura déterminé pendant le cours, que vous allez annoncer d'emblée et qui vous aura permis d'établir votre plan.
- **Parlez de documents** étudiés en classe en rapport avec l'angle choisi (seuls les élèves de la série L pourront les avoir sous les yeux) afin d'étayer et d'illustrer votre propos. Veillez à toujours préciser la nature du document évoqué (texte, document visuel, audio ou vidéo) et à employer le lexique approprié pour le décrire brièvement et pour expliciter le message de l'auteur. Cela dit, n'essayez pas de faire allusion à trop de documents lors de votre présentation (trois ou quatre documents semblent être un maximum raisonnable) car il s'agit de présenter une notion ; il faut privilégier la démonstration. En outre, vous ne disposerez que de 5 ou 10 minutes de temps de parole.
- **Ajoutez des références tirées de votre expérience personnelle** pour enrichir votre présentation et **n'hésitez pas à donner votre opinion**.

ZOOM

Quelques outils pour parler des documents

▶ Introduire

The topic of my presentation today is... • I'm going to speak about... • I'd like to focus on a specific aspect, which is... • More precisely, I'm going to deal with... • On the one hand... on the other hand... : d'une part..., d'autre part...
In addition, ...
In contrast

▶ Parler des documents

The first document is a passage from a novel / an excerpt from a short story / a cartoon / a comic strip / an ad(vertisement) / a photo(graph) / a painting / a still / a film poster : le premier document est un passage tiré d'un roman / un extrait de nouvelle / un dessin humoristique / une BD / une publicité / une photo / un tableau / une photo de film / une affiche de cinéma.

The next document is an interview / a conversation / a speech / a monologue / a poem / a report / an extract from a documentary / a passage from a film.

It shows... : il représente...

It is about...

deliver a message : transmettre un message

besides : en outre

however : cependant

nevertheless : néanmoins

The author may have tried to imply that... / to criticise / to denounce / to symbolise / to make fun of... : L'auteur a peut-être essayé de suggérer que... / de critiquer / de dénoncer / de symboliser / de se moquer de...

▶ Conclure

As far as... is / are concerned : En ce qui concerne...

This reminds me of... / This makes me think of... : Cela me rappelle ... / Cela me fait penser à ...

As for me : Quant à moi

I, for one, would say that... : Personnellement, je dirais que...

To conclude, ...

RÉCAPITULONS

- La prise de parole en continu est la première partie de l'épreuve d'expression orale et porte majoritairement sur l'étude des notions au programme.
- La préparation à cet exercice doit être régulière et porter aussi bien sur le fond que sur la forme, étant donné qu'il s'agit d'un acte de communication.
- La présentation de la notion se fait dans une perspective déterminée au cours du travail en classe en faisant référence à des documents variés.

Présenter une notion

LA DÉMARCHE

- Je dois traiter une notion en m'appuyant sur **plusieurs documents**.
- J'ai à l'esprit les **principaux enjeux** que recouvre cette notion.
- Je pense à adopter une **attitude propice à une bonne communication** et à employer le lexique et les structures appropriées.

L'EXEMPLE COMMENTÉ

Présenter la notion « L'idée de progrès »

DOCUMENT 1

Faster, Higher, Poppa: the best Olympian of all

For the creator of the Paralympics the Games were about overcoming – first the Nazis, then disability.

“My favourite Olympian was small, short-sighted and tubby. He could not run fast, swim or jump. He smoked a pipe and everyone called him 'Poppa'. There is no evidence he ever participated in any form of competitive sport. But he profoundly understood, and changed, the meaning of the Olympic Games.

His name was Ludwig Guttmann; he was a pioneering German-Jewish neurosurgeon and he invented the Paralympics. Guttmann knew that sport is not just about 'faster, higher, stronger', but about overcoming limitations, extending the physically possible, and the extraordinary psychological benefit of sporting aspiration. He applied that understanding to the bodies and minds of men broken on the battlefields of the Second World War, and in so doing he helped to revolutionise modern attitudes towards disabilities.

Poppa Guttmann knew all about overcoming adversity. Born in a mining town in Upper Silesia in 1899 he worked after school in a hospital. [...]

As a medical student at Freiburg, Guttmann noticed the way that Jewish fraternities dedicated to sport gave their members extraordinary confidence and self-esteem. [...]

Olympian: personne associée aux Jeux olympiques
Jewish neurosurgeon: neuro-chirurgien juif
overcome: vaincre
confidence: confiance

He became director of the neurological department of Breslau Jewish Hospital, but by 1939 the Gestapo was closing in. He managed to smuggle most of his patients out of the hospital before they were rounded up, and then fled himself. Guttmann arrived at Harwich with his wife and children in March 1939.

The British medical establishment was quick to utilise his remarkable talents and in 1943 Guttmann was made director of a new spinal injuries centre at Stoke Mandeville, a hospital created in preparation for the expected casualties from the opening of the Second Front. At that time, the life expectancy of spinal-injury patients was two years.

Over the next five years, Guttmann treated hundreds of wounded and paralysed soldiers. His programme aimed to reintegrate these disabled men and women into normal British life and he placed particular emphasis on sport, both as physical rehabilitation but also as a path to rediscovering self-discipline, self-respect and team spirit. [...]

On July 28, 1948, 16 former soldiers (including two women) with spinal injuries gathered in wheelchairs on the lawn outside the Stoke Mandeville wards for an archery competition.

By 1952 the "Stoke Mandeville Games" had 130 international competitors; in 1960 the first Paralympic Games (the name was applied retrospectively) were held in Rome. [...]

Poppa Guttmann ran a long, hard race against prejudice, but he won in the end.

The Times, July 13, 2012.

smuggle: faire passer clandestinement
spinal injuries: blessures à la colonne vertébrale
life expectancy: espérance de vie
emphasis: accent, insistance
archery: tir à l'arc

DOCUMENT 2

"AFTER THE BIG RACE THE TORTOISE AND THE HARE ARE ORDERED TO PROVIDE URINE SAMPLES"

DOCUMENT 3

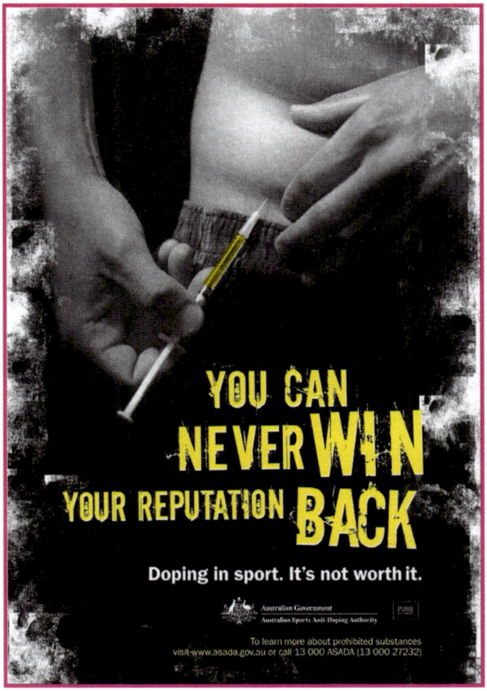

Introduction

POUR VOUS AIDER
Cette introduction pose la problématique, donc l'angle d'attaque.

- **Idée de progrès :** liée à notion de développement + volonté d'amélioration (plan individuel + collectif).
- **Sport :** discipline pour se dépasser. Cependant les records à battre : de plus en plus élevés → certains athlètes oublient les idéaux sportifs.

The notion of progress implies improvement and betterment individually as well as collectively. This is what sport is about, but as athletes want to break higher and higher records, they sometimes tend to ignore prevalent notions like team spirit, self-discipline and fair play.

Étude des documents

• **Trois documents pour illustrer cette notion :** extrait d'article de presse sur l'origine des Jeux paralympiques, dessin humoristique sur les contrôles médicaux (lutte contre le dopage), publicité (campagne australienne contre le dopage).

The three documents that can help illustrate the notion of progress are first, a press article from the *Times*, a British newspaper, giving a short biography of Ludwig Guttmann, the creator of the Paralympics, secondly a cartoon about the medical tests sometimes performed after a race, and lastly a photograph from an Australian awareness campaign against doping launched by the Australian Sports Anti-Doping Authority (ASADA) and targeting athletes and their support staff.

POUR VOUS AIDER
La nature des documents est spécifiée mais leur description reste brève.

• **Progrès médical :** au service de l'humain (voir documents 1 et 2)

• **Document 1** : rôle et influence de Ludwig Guttmann : progrès médical → dignité des personnes ayant souffert physiquement et mentalement + changement des mentalités à l'égard du handicap + (re)donner un rôle social aux personnes handicapées.

• **Document 2** : rôle de la médecine : garantir le bon déroulement des compétitions en testant les sportifs. Humour (voir fable d'Esope puis de La Fontaine) + message : victoire douteuse de la tortue (résultat d'une tricherie ?) mais rapidité du lièvre également suspecte.

On the one hand, medical advances appear to be beneficial to human life. This is what Ludwig Guttmann's life and work tend to imply. As a Jewish doctor who had to flee Nazi Germany, he devoted his life to helping soldiers wounded during World War II regain their dignity, self-reliance, and a sense of purpose in society. By making these disabled soldiers do sport again and participate in competitions, he also contributed to a change in mentalities within the whole society.

In document 2, we are reminded that the role of medical science is also to ensure that the competing athletes do not cheat by testing them. The amusing allusion to the fable nonetheless denounces a serious issue, namely cheating through doping. The tortoise and the hare are both suspected and scientists are there to look for evidence of doping.

- **Avancées en médecine toujours positives ?**

(Par exemple : découverte de nouveaux médicaments à des fins nocives et malhonnêtes) ≠ esprit olympique / Ludwig Guttmann.

- **Document 2** : lièvre et tortue déconcertés → quelque chose à cacher.
- **Document 3** : campagne de sensibilisation contre le dopage (traitement plus sérieux) → dégradation morale due à l'utilisation de produits même si victoire = gloire pour un temps.

Although science enables society to unmask and punish cheats, it also provides them with steroids and other drugs. It thus helps dishonest people while ruining their health. This is what the hare and the tortoise's looks suggest in the cartoon.
However the last document, which shows an athlete injecting himself, delivers a very serious message. Doping damages a reputation and therefore can potentially mean the end of a career.
Therefore, doping is indeed not worth it, as stated in the slogan of the campaign.

Conclusion

Progrès (connaissances médicales) n'a pas toujours des effets positifs (voir domaine du sport). Médecine : aide pour les personnes handicapées (exploits sportifs) mais dopage = danger (santé + réputation) → nécessité de contrôle éthique du progrès scientifique.

Progress does not always mean improvement, especially in medical science. Even though more and more disabled people can have access to better living conditions, medical research is not always applied for honest purposes. Scientists who enable athletes to use drugs to enhance their performances are like sorcerer's apprentices. Dr Seward, a character in Bram Stoker's *Dracula*, says that "there may be a poison that distils itself out good things" – that's why the notion of progress involves controlling and checking, and depends on ethics.

SE TESTER QUIZ

1 Utiliser le bon niveau de langue

Parmi ces expressions et fragments de phrases, cochez ceux qui ne sont pas souhaitables dans une présentation orale. Puis donnez un équivalent plus approprié.

- ☐ **1.** Like I said… ....
- ☐ **2.** This document is really awesome. ....
- ☐ **3.** The author implies that… ....
- ☐ **4.** The character feels like he wants to run away. ....
- ☐ **5.** I firmly believe that… ....
- ☐ **6.** I'm pretty impressed by this document. ....
- ☐ **7.** It is kind of scary. ....
- ☐ **8.** This advertisement is extremely effective. ....

S'ENTRAÎNER

2 Préparer ses notes

Lisez les documents suivants qui vous permettront de présenter la notion « Lieux et formes du pouvoir » et, sous forme de notes brèves, suivez ces étapes :

1. Donnez la nature, la source, la date et l'auteur (s'il est précisé) de chaque document.
2. Indiquez les thèmes communs à ces trois documents.
3. Proposez une problématique (rappelez la notion étudiée tout en y rattachant un angle d'attaque précis). Puis suggérez un plan.

DOCUMENT 1

“In Stamps the segregation was so complete that most Black children didn't really, absolutely know what whites looked like. Other than they were different, to be dreaded, and in that dread was included the hostility of the powerless against the powerful, the poor against the rich, the worker against the worked for and the ragged against the well-dressed.

Maya Angelou, *I Know Why the Caged Bird Sings*, 1969.

Stamps: ville de l'Arkansas où sévissait la ségrégation dans les années 1930, période pendant laquelle se passe l'action
other than: si ce n'est que
dread: redouter
the ragged: les miséreux en haillons

DOCUMENT 2

© Steve Sack

POUR VOUS AIDER
Ce dessin humoristique a été publié peu après l'élection de Barack Obama en 2008.

DOCUMENT 3

“ **Blacks Miss out as Jobs Rebound in New York City** by Patrick McGeehan

highlight: souligner
a downturn: une baisse
a résumé: un C.V.
land a job: get a job

For months now, New York officials have been highlighting how the city has regained all the jobs lost during the long recession and then some. But by several measures, the city's recovery has left black New Yorkers behind.

More than half of all of African-Americans and other non-Hispanic blacks in the city who were old enough to work had no job at all this year, according to an analysis of employment data compiled by the federal Labor Department. And when black New Yorkers lose their jobs, they spend a full year, on average, trying to find new jobs – far longer than New Yorkers of other races. […]

One problem, said David R. Jones, the president and chief executive of the Community Service Society of New York, is that blacks were overrepresented in fields that suffered the most in the downturn, including government agencies, construction and manufacturing. […]

Latoya Ingram, 33, who lives in Harlem, said she had been looking for full-time work since 2009.

In that time, she said, she had sent off more than 1,000 copies of her résumé.

Unlike some other unemployed New Yorkers interviewed, Ms Ingram, who is black and earned a bachelor's degree in marketing from Syracuse University in 2001, said she believed her race was a factor in her inability to land a job.

"I could be wrong, but I've had interviews, and they seem really, really interested," she said.

"Then they see me in person and they're not that interested," added Ms Ingram who has been collecting $215 a week in unemployment benefits. "I think it's a combination of being black and overweight: they think you are lazy."

The *New York Times*, June 20, 2012.

OBJECTIF BAC

3 Présenter une notion

Présentez la notion « Lieux et formes du pouvoir » à travers ces trois documents.

SE TESTER

1 1. *Like I said…* : inapproprié même si on l'entend souvent dans des conversations. *Like* est une préposition et doit être suivi d'un groupe nominal et non d'un groupe verbal. Il faut dire *As I said…*

2. *This document is really awesome* : *awesome* est un adjectif passe-partout qui pourrait être l'équivalent de « super, génial » en français. Il faut donc le remplacer par un adjectif plus original et significatif, comme *impressive* ou *outstanding* (remarquable).

3. *The author implies that…* : expression correcte.

4. *The character feels like he wants to run away* : inapproprié pour la même raison que dans la phrase 1. Ici, il faut remplacer *like* par *as if* et mettre le verbe *want* au prétérit de l'irréel. La phrase correcte donne : *The character feels as if he wanted to run away.*

5. *I firmly believe that…* : énoncé de bonne qualité, à privilégier.

6. *I'm pretty impressed by this document* : l'adverbe *pretty* est un équivalent familier de *fairly*. Il a sa place dans une conversation mais pas lors d'un oral en continu.

7. *It is kind of scary* : *kind of* est une autre expression familière qu'il faut remplacer par un adverbe tel que *slightly* (légèrement) ou *somewhat* (quelque peu).

8. *This advertisement is extremely effective* : énoncé correct.

S'ENTRAÎNER

2 1. The first document is a short passage from Maya Angelou's novel *I Know Why the Caged Bird Sings* in which the narrator recalls her life during segregation in Alabama, a southern State.
The second document is a cartoon published in an American newspaper The *Star Tribune*, after Barack Obama's first election in 2008.
The third one is a recent article from The *New York Times* and highlights the fact that African Americans find it difficult to get jobs in New York while the recession seems to be over for most communities.

2. These three documents deal with the African-American community at different times during the 20th century until now. They remind us that the road to power has been a long and bumpy one despite Barack Obama's first victory, and that they still have to fight for equality.

3. Studying "Seats and Forms of Power" means studying the various struggles that have given American Blacks more power. The USA and especially the Deep South have always been the arch places of the African-American fight for more power.
First part: Segregation, which followed slavery, still deprived the black community of any form of power in the South.
Second part: This led to forms of resistance and protest, which made the dream of equality and power come true.
Third part: In some areas, however, racial discrimination is still showing its ugly head.

OBJECTIF BAC

3 • Après l'abolition de l'esclavage en 1865 (13e Amendement de la Constitution des États-Unis), pour laquelle Abraham Lincoln a œuvré, la ségrégation dans les États du Sud a permis la réaffirmation du pouvoir des Blancs en séparant les deux communautés et en privant les Noirs de droits fondamentaux. À la lecture du premier document, on perçoit cette séparation encore vivace dans les années 1930, et on voit que cette forme de pouvoir exercée par les Blancs entraînait un profond ressentiment chez les Noirs.

Slavery was abolished in 1865. Abraham Lincoln (Document 2) is remembered as the champion of this cause. However the Southern States gradually managed to deprive black people of their rights by setting up a series of segregation laws (Jim Crow Laws) to ensure white power.

The passage by Maya Angelou (Document 1) makes it clear that the two communities are estranged and that "the powerless" fear "the powerful".

• L'élection de Barack Obama a couronné le combat de résistance des années 1950 et 1960. Dans le dessin humoristique, les deux présidents, issus de deux communautés différentes, semblent néanmoins montrer une grande complicité et Lincoln, souriant, félicite Obama qui se retrouve à la tête de l'État. L'endroit est aussi très symbolique : le *Lincoln Memorial* se trouve à Washington, D.C., lieu du pouvoir suprême. La symbolique de leur geste (un salut entre membres d'une même bande) est également importante : il signifie qu'Obama a prolongé le combat de Lincoln pour que les Afro-Américains accèdent au pouvoir politique.

This struggle for political power symbolically ended with the election and reelection of Barack Obama who, as the 44th president, thus became the first African American to hold the office. The cartoon shows him with Abraham Lincoln at the Lincoln Memorial in Washington, D.C. They are doing a fist bump and smiling at each other, which means that they are really proud of what they have achieved for the African-American community: freeing the slaves on the one hand and being elected president on the other. Even though they clearly stand for each community (Lincoln's statue is white whereas Obama is dressed in black) their gesture unites them.

• Cependant, la lutte pour les lieux et les formes du pouvoir est un éternel recommencement : le pouvoir économique des Afro-Américains n'est pas encore tout à fait établi. Dans l'article, on apprend que les Afro-Américains à New York rencontrent des difficultés à retrouver un emploi dans une ville qui se remet peu à peu de la crise, alors que les autres communautés n'ont pas ce problème.

However this dream of equality is only starting to become a reality as all the seats and forms of power have not yet been conquered by African-Americans. According to the article, African-Americans today are not the masters of their fate as they find it difficult to get jobs in New York after the economic slump, unlike other people from other communities. For instance, a young woman who graduated from university is convinced that she is racially discriminated against (Document 3).

• Ces trois documents illustrent certaines étapes de la relation au pouvoir de la communauté noire américaine. De citoyens de seconde zone, ils sont devenus citoyens à part entière. Mais les préjugés persistent. Le combat pour le pouvoir économique, notamment, n'est certainement pas terminé.

Through these three documents, it is possible to see how the access to power has evolved for the African-American community. From second-class citizens they have become full-fledged citizens. But there is still a long way to go in many fields to become more powerful.

CHAPITRE

10 S'exprimer à l'oral en interaction

Cet exercice constitue la seconde partie de l'épreuve d'expression orale au baccalauréat et consiste en un échange avec le professeur ou l'examinateur (selon les filières) devant lequel vous venez de présenter une des notions du programme. Ce dialogue va s'appuyer sur votre présentation (→ chapitre 9).

I Description de l'épreuve

- La **durée** de cette seconde partie de l'épreuve varie selon la filière choisie (5, 10 ou 20 minutes).
- Les **questions posées** sont en rapport avec la présentation que vous venez d'effectuer et vous inviteront, la plupart du temps, à préciser et clarifier ce que vous avez dit dans la première partie, mais aussi à développer tel ou tel aspect de la question en donnant des exemples.
- Ce moment d'interaction doit aussi vous permettre de parler de votre **expérience personnelle**.

II S'entraîner à la prise de parole en interaction

A À la maison

Joignez l'utile à l'agréable ! Lorsque vous regardez une série ou un film, faites-le en version originale. Pendant les conversations entre les personnages, soyez actif et essayez de repérer les expressions idiomatiques caractéristiques du dialogue : donner son opinion, exprimer son accord ou son désaccord, hésiter, insister, répéter les paroles de l'interlocuteur… L'idéal est de les noter dans un carnet et de s'entraîner à les répéter.

B En classe

Pensez dès cette année à participer de manière active en classe et à réagir à la parole des autres, élèves comme professeur. Cela vous permettra d'acquérir de l'authenticité et de ne plus appréhender l'examen oral. Cet entraînement nécessite bien sûr d'être extrêmement attentif à tout ce qui se dit pendant le cours. Voici quelques règles simples à suivre.

Attitude

- Soyez plus naturel que lors d'un exposé formel. Lors de l'entretien, vous pouvez utiliser le « langage du corps ».
- Parlez distinctement en ayant soin de regarder votre interlocuteur.

Qualité linguistique

- Utilisez un niveau de langue courant. Votre échange est beaucoup moins formel que pendant une prise de parole en continu, mais variez les expressions pour être sûr d'avoir été bien compris. Si ce n'est pas le cas, on pourra vous demander des éclaircissements.
- Évitez de répondre uniquement par *yes* ou *no* lorsqu'on vous pose une question. Il faut utiliser des réponses courtes avec reprise d'auxiliaire ou des expressions toutes faites.

Contenu

- N'hésitez pas à développer votre point de vue et à affirmer votre position.
- Votre temps de parole doit être supérieur à celui du professeur / examinateur.

Pour ne pas « sécher »

- Soyez très concentré mais vous pouvez demander de répéter en anglais ce qui vient d'être dit si vous n'avez pas bien compris ou entendu.
- Employez aussi des *gap fillers*, ces petits mots ou expressions qui vous donnent le temps de réfléchir. En effet, il est davantage accepté d'hésiter qu'en prise de parole en continu.

POUR SE DONNER LE TEMPS DE LA RÉFLEXION

Let me see / think...
What I mean is...
I see what you mean...
Well, you may be right but...
You know... / You see...

ZOOM

Répondre de manière authentique

Pour insister

- Emploi des auxiliaires *do* et *did*

  "You don't love me, Eva." "What? I do love you, you know I do."

- Emploi des *question tags*

  "This woman went down in history." "Yes, she did, didn't she?"

  "Politicians shouldn't overlook this crisis." "No, they shouldn't, should they?"

Pour ne pas répéter

- Reprise par l'auxiliaire

  "Do you often use the Internet?" "Yes, I do."

  "Have you got several computers at home?" "No, I haven't."

- Reprise par *so* ou *not*

  Is this a burning issue?
  I think so. ≠ I think not.
  I suppose so. ≠ I suppose not.
  I guess so. ≠ I guess not.

  Will books disappear soon?
  Of course! ≠ Of course not!
  I hope so. ≠ I hope not.
  I'm afraid so. ≠ I'm afraid not.

Pour exprimer son accord / désaccord

- Reprise par l'auxiliaire

  "This artist draws like a four-year-old." "No, he doesn't!"

  "Western countries didn't react." "Yes, they did!"

- Emploi d'expressions idiomatiques

  I do agree with... — Quite right! — That's exactly what I mean!
  That's true! — Sure! — Indeed!

RÉCAPITULONS

- La prise de parole en interaction est la seconde partie de l'épreuve d'expression orale et constitue un prolongement de la présentation.
- La préparation à cet exercice doit être régulière pendant le cours. Mais il est possible aussi de vous entraîner pendant votre temps libre.
- L'entretien avec l'examinateur doit être animé et le plus authentique possible.

S'entretenir avec le professeur / examinateur

LA DÉMARCHE

- Je dois adopter une **attitude respectueuse mais décidée**.
- Je **réponds aux questions** en gardant la parole le plus longtemps possible grâce à des éléments et des exemples nouveaux.
- J'emploie des expressions idiomatiques propres à la **langue orale**.

L'EXEMPLE COMMENTÉ

- Le dialogue suivant est une simulation d'interaction qui pourrait suivre la présentation sur l'idée de progrès proposée au chapitre 9 (→ p. 95-99).
- Vous pouvez écouter cet échange sur le site www.prepabac.com/media.

POUR VOUS AIDER

- Les expressions pour éviter la répétition sont en bleu.
- Les *gap fillers* sont en vert.
- Les formules d'insistance sont en rouge.

TEACHER: You've mentioned a few positive values associated with sport, like fair play, team spirit. Can you think of others?

STUDENT: Of course. Let me see… Sport teaches you control and does teach you how to use the rules you've learnt in a particular sport in real life. Actually, I would say that sport turns out to be really useful in your daily life.

TEACHER: Do you do any sport?

STUDENT: Yes, I do. I play tennis as an extracurricular activity and obviously, I have P.E. at school.

TEACHER: Has playing tennis, then, taught you anything?

STUDENT: I hope so! Well, sure. It has taught me to focus on what I'm doing – as a matter of fact a match can last for ages you know – and to control myself – I mustn't get too nervous or flustered you see… if I lose three points in a row.

TEACHER: All right. So much for the positive values of sport. Let's talk about the problem of doping. Can you think of a recent example of a sportsman ending his career because of that?

STUDENT: **Yes, of course.** There's Lance Armstrong, who decided in Summer 2012 to stop his cycling career altogether. Whether he was guilty and did not deserve to be called a champion or not, I think he should be looked up to...

TEACHER: Should he?

STUDENT: **Oh yes, he should. Why shouldn't he? Indeed**, people should admire him for the good fight he fought against cancer. Speaking of guilt, I remember reading an article about another great athlete... **um... let me think of his name... yes...** Dwain Chambers. He used to be a doper himself and just before the 2012 Olympics, he warned sportsmen and women against doping saying "if testers don't get you guilt will."

TEACHER: Why do you think he said such a thing?

STUDENT: **Well...** most certainly, he couldn't stand being a cheat and a liar, so when he got tested he must have been relieved and now he wants his experience to serve as an example. So I think that the saying "every cloud has a silver lining" does apply to Chambers. Because of this very traumatic experience he's become a better person. Sport has taught him a moral lesson.

TEACHER: Then sport teaches people many things about life.

STUDENT: **Yes, it does, doesn't it?**

TEACHER: Well, thank you.

STUDENT: My pleasure!

POUR VOUS AIDER

- Vous constatez que lors de cet échange, seules onze lignes sont consacrées à la transcription des paroles prononcées par la professeure, alors que l'élève parle deux fois plus.
- L'examinatrice reprend méthodiquement les points abordés par la présentation de la notion (→ p. 95-99).

SE TESTER QUIZ

1 Employer des réponses courtes

Cochez la réponse la plus appropriée à chaque question dans le cadre de l'épreuve.

1. Have you ever joined a charity?
- ☐ **a.** Yes. ☐ **b.** Yes, I have.

2. Can you give the names of two major American presidents?
- ☐ **a.** I'm afraid I can't. ☐ **b.** No, sorry.

3. Has this technology got many advantages?
- ☐ **a.** I hope it has. ☐ **b.** I hope it has many advantages.

4. Is this hero your favourite one?
- ☐ **a.** I think that he is my favourite. ☐ **b.** I think so.

5. Would it be good to stop creating boundaries *(frontières)*?
- ☐ **a.** I'm afraid not. ☐ **b.** No, it wouldn't be a good idea.

6. Do you think that "the pen is mightier than the sword"?
- ☐ **a.** Yes, I do. ☐ **b.** Yes, the pen is.

S'ENTRAÎNER

2 Employer des *question tags*

Complétez les phrases suivantes avec le *question tag* qui convient.

1. He is the fastest man on earth, ...?
2. She wasn't aware of the power of advertising, ...?
3. We must begin to consume less energy, ...?
4. These stars hit the headlines, ...?
5. They hadn't been involved in a scandal before, ...?
6. He should have hired a lawyer in the first place, ...?

OBJECTIF BAC

3 Répondre aux questions de l'examinateur

Vous avez présenté la notion « Lieux et formes du pouvoir » à l'aide d'un extrait du roman de Maya Angelou *(I Know Why the Caged Bird Sings)*, d'un dessin humoristique sur l'élection d'Obama et d'un article du *New York Times* sur le chômage des Afro-Américains à New York (→ p. 100-102).

Lisez les questions ci-dessous qu'un examinateur pourrait vous poser à la suite de cette présentation puis répondez-y.

POUR VOUS AIDER

- Pensez à des réponses possibles pour ces questions. Songez à développer vos réponses.
- Écoutez l'enregistrement de ces questions sur le site et après chacune d'entre elles, proposez une réponse en temps réel. N'oubliez pas les réponses courtes, les *question tags* et les formules d'insistance.

1. Why did segregation happen in the South?
2. Have you studied any other text by Maya Angelou?
3. Can you name and talk about a few people who fought against segregation?
4. Are you interested in US politics?
5. What kind of protest do you find the most effective?
6. What cause would you be ready to defend?

SE TESTER

1 1. **b.** Yes, I have.
2. **a.** I'm afraid I can't.
3. **a.** I hope it has.
4. **b.** I think so.
5. **a.** I'm afraid not.
6. **a.** Yes, I do. (Ici, la question porte sur l'opinion de l'interlocuteur, non sur la proposition subordonnée introduite par *that*.)

S'ENTRAÎNER

2 1. … isn't he?
2. … was she?
3. … mustn't we?
4. … didn't they?
5. … had they?
6. … shouldn't he?

OBJECTIF BAC

3 Proposition de corrigé

1. Of course, former slave owners were against the abolition of slavery. That's why they decided to limit black people's rights. Segregation was soon implemented in the South after the Federal Supreme Court declared the practice constitutional since the former slaves were "separate but equal".
2. Yes, I have. Actually, I have studied several poems. The one I remember well is *Still I Rise*. It appeals to me because her words are extremely forceful in this poem, aren't they? The whole poem is about the way black slaves were oppressed in America and about the way they managed to free themselves.
3. Yes, I can. The most famous one was of course Martin Luther King Jr. He was a baptist minister and advocated non-violence and integration. That's why he called for a boycott of public buses in Montgomery after Rosa Parks was arrested. His numerous speeches are well-known. On the other hand, people like Malcolm X were more likely to be aggressive towards the white community and believed in black nationalism.
4. Of course I am. I do think you can't do without the USA today. Actually I rather support…
5. I definitely disapprove of violent means. You see, people like Martin Luther King Jr. are my greatest heroes. They never used violence to stand up against injustice. In addition, I believe that art can sometimes be an effective way to open people's eyes on such and such issue.
6. Well, let me think. I'm afraid there are too many causes to defend. Yet I do think I would give money for medical research or for the cause of women all over the world. These are rather good choices, aren't they?

Grammaire

CHAPITRE

11 Les articles et les démonstratifs

Les articles *the*, *a(n)*, *Ø* (= article « zéro ») et les démonstratifs *this* et *that* (pluriels : *these* et *those*) déterminent le sens ou la portée des noms. Ainsi : *Ø Cats love Ø milk* ne signifie pas la même chose que : *The cats love Ø milk*, ou encore : *The cats love the milk*. De même, *this morning* et *that morning* ne sont pas synonymes.
Pour ne pas se tromper d'article, il est important de savoir si le nom est dénombrable ou non (→ p. 144-146).

I L'article *a (an)*

■ *A (an)* est **toujours suivi d'un nom dénombrable singulier**.

He is an idiot and a snob.

ATTENTION !
A s'emploie devant une consonne et devant ***u*** et ***eu*** prononcés /jʊ/ ou /juː/.
An s'emploie devant une voyelle et devant le ***h*** muet : *heir* (héritier), *honest, hour, honour* (→ p. 76).

■ *A (an)* est **obligatoire après un nom dénombrable singulier** :

- pour renseigner sur une **profession**

  She is **a** teacher and he is **an** architect.
  Elle est Ø enseignante et il est Ø architecte.

- après ***without***

  He went out without **an** umbrella.
  Il est sorti sans Ø parapluie.

- après ***what*** et ***such*** dans les exclamatives

  What **a** lovely day! / It's such **a** lovely day!
  Quelle Ø belle journée !

• dans les structures **appositives**

Edith Wharton, **a** famous American novelist, lived here for several years.
Edith Wharton, Ø célèbre romancière américaine, vécut ici pendant plusieurs années.

■ *A (an)* peut être **distributif**.

He goes to the USA twice **a** month.
Il se rend aux États-Unis deux fois par mois.

II L'article *the*

■ *The* peut être associé à tous les types de noms : dénombrables et indénombrables.

Look! **The** dog has found something.
Regarde ! **Le** chien a trouvé quelque chose.

Ada is not here. She is walking **the** dogs.
Ada n'est pas là. Elle promène **les** chiens.

The people we met were very helpful.
Les gens que nous avons rencontrés étaient très serviables.

The love she shows towards me leaves me cold.
L'amour qu'elle me témoigne me laisse froid.

■ « Le », « la », « les » ne se traduisent pas forcément par *the*. L'utilisation de *the* est souvent justifiée par le contexte, la situation, la réalité culturelle.

• **Contexte**

Ø Doctors do a fabulous job.
Les médecins font un travail formidable. (généralité)

The doctors **I met** were very competent.
Les médecins que j'ai rencontrés étaient très compétents. (ceux-là spécifiquement)

• **Situation**

I'd like to visit **the** museum.
Je voudrais visiter le musée. (de la ville où je me trouve)

Pass me **the** salt, please.
Passe-moi le sel, s'il te plaît. (le sel qui est sur la table)

• **Réalité culturelle**

The Prince laughed.
Le Prince a ri. (On sait quel prince.)

The sun and **the** moon and **the** earth…
(aucune ambiguïté possible)

ATTENTION !
The Prince laughed. (titre seul = *the*)
Mais : Ø Prince Charles is bald. (titre + nom = Ø) Le Prince Charles est chauve.

- *The* s'emploie aussi devant les adjectifs substantivés (= nominalisés) (→ p. 156).

  Life must be difficult for the blind.
  La vie doit être difficile pour les aveugles.

- L'article *the* s'emploie obligatoirement :

• devant des noms pluriels renvoyant à des groupes humains : famille, nationalité, catégorie sociale, culturelle.

  Meet **the** Dicksons.
  Je vous présente les Dickson.

  The French are said to be proud of their past.
  On dit que les Français sont fiers de leur passé.

  The Republicans abolished slavery in 1863.
  Les Républicains ont aboli l'esclavage en 1863.

• devant les noms d'instruments de musique (anglais britannique).

  He plays **the** violin.

• devant les noms de cours d'eau, fleuves, mers, chaînes de montagnes (mais pas devant les noms de lacs ou de sommets montagneux).

  We went to **the** Himalayas to climb **Ø** Mount Everest.

• devant les noms de certains pays formés à partir de noms communs.

  the United States (of America)
  the Netherlands (les Pays-Bas)
  the United Kingdom
  Attention : **Ø** Great Britain.

• devant *school, hospital, church, prison, jail, cinema, theatre,* etc. lorsqu'ils désignent les bâtiments.

  We went to **the** cinema last night. (bâtiment)
  We love **Ø** cinema. (l'art cinématographique)

III L'article « zéro » (Ø)

- Avec les dénombrables pluriels et les indénombrables, l'article « zéro » (Ø) signifie **« le », « la », « les » en général**.

  I like **Ø** horses.
  J'aime les chevaux. (en général)

  Ø Love makes the world go round.
  C'est l'amour qui mène le monde.

L'article Ø équivaut aussi à **« du », « de la », « des »**. Il permet avec des dénombrables pluriels et des indénombrables de « prélever » une partie d'un ensemble.

I had **Ø** meat, **Ø** vegetables and **Ø** chocolate cake.
J'ai mangé **de** la viande, **des** légumes et **du** gâteau au chocolat.

ZOOM

A, the ou Ø ?

	dénombrables singuliers	dénombrables pluriels	indénombrables
a(n)	He gave me **a** watch.		
the	I like **the** watch he gave me.	**The** books she writes are funny.	**The** tea you drink here is excellent.
Ø		She writes **Ø** books.	He likes **Ø** tea.

IV Les démonstratifs

singulier	pluriel	singulier	pluriel
this	these	that	those

Fonctions des démonstratifs

Les démonstratifs peuvent être déterminants d'un nom, d'un groupe nominal ou du pronom *one*.

Have you read **this** newspaper?
Tu as lu ce journal ?

If you can carry **those** plates, I'll take **these**.
Si tu peux prendre ces assiettes, je prends celles-ci.

ATTENTION !

Notez aussi l'utilisation de *this / that* dans des énoncés qui soulignent le degré ou l'ordre de grandeur de quelque chose.

He was wearing a cap and was about **this** tall.
Il portait une casquette et il était à peu près grand comme ça.

This / these : le proche, *that / those* : le lointain

This (pluriel : *these*) est utilisé pour ce qui est proche, *that* (pluriel : *those*) pour ce qui est éloigné. Cette proximité ou cet éloignement peuvent être d'ordre spatial, temporel ou affectif.

proximité dans l'espace : *this / these*	**éloignement dans l'espace : *that / those***
We have two paintings by Picasso. **This** one **here**... Nous avons deux toiles de Picasso. Celle-ci (près de moi)...	... and **that** one on the **opposite wall**. ... et celle-là sur le mur d'en face.
This is Kate, my sister... Je te présente ma sœur, Kate...	... and **that** lady **over there** is our mother. ... et cette dame là-bas est notre mère.
proximité dans le temps : *this / these*	**éloignement dans le temps : *that / those***
This is a great year... Cette année est formidable...	... not like **2006! That year was** awful! ... pas comme 2006 ! Cette année-là fut horrible !
proximité affective : *this / these*	**éloignement affectif : *that / those***
Give some toys to **these** children. Donne des jouets à ces (gentils) enfants.	Who are **those** children? Qui sont ces (sales) gamins ?

DÉMONSTRATIFS ET TEMPS

Notez que *this / these* renvoient au présent ou au futur tandis que *that / those* renvoient au passé.

The weather has been gorgeous **this** week.
Le temps est splendide cette semaine.

People died young in **those** days.
Les gens mouraient jeunes à cette époque.

This / That renvoyant à du texte ou à des paroles

• En général, ***that*** reprend ce qui vient d'être dit.

He said he spent hours on his essay, but that's a lie.
Il dit qu'il a passé des heures sur son devoir mais c'est faux.

Sorry, I wasn't listening. Could you say that again, please?
Désolée, je n'écoutais pas. Tu peux répéter, s'il te plaît ?

• Le plus souvent, ***this*** annonce, présente ce qui suit.

"And let me tell you this: we'll find the culprit," he said.
« Et laisse-moi te dire une chose : on trouvera le coupable », dit-il.

• Cependant, ***this*** peut reprendre ce qui vient d'être dit ou écrit, si le locuteur annonce un développement.

The main character of the novel is very pessimistic. **This** is shown right from the beginning of the book.
Le personnage principal du roman est très pessimiste. Cela se voit dès le début du livre.

RÉCAPITULONS

- *A(n)* s'emploie surtout avec des noms dénombrables au singulier.
- **L'article dit « zéro » (Ø)** s'emploie essentiellement avec des dénombrables au pluriel ou avec des indénombrables.
- ***The*** fonctionne avec les dénombrables et les indénombrables.
- Seuls les démonstratifs ***this*** ou ***that*** peuvent accompagner des indénombrables puisque ceux-ci sont toujours singuliers.

SE TESTER QUIZ

1 **Choisissez la bonne réponse.**

1. Lisa doesn't want to go to ... university next year.
- ☐ **a.** an ☐ **b.** a ☐ **c.** Ø

2. What ... awful weather! It's been raining all day.
- ☐ **a.** Ø ☐ **b.** the ☐ **c.** an

3. . ... painting by Hopper I like best is *Nighthawks*.
- ☐ **a.** The ☐ **b.** A ☐ **c.** Ø

4. They have built ... hospital on the island.
- ☐ **a.** Ø ☐ **b.** a ☐ **c.** an

5. Mark's brother is in ... jail again.
- ☐ **a.** the ☐ **b.** a ☐ **c.** Ø

6. What? You want to marry ... stupid woman? You must be mad!
- ☐ **a.** this ☐ **b.** the ☐ **c.** that

7. And let me tell you ... : we shall win!
- ☐ **a.** that ☐ **b.** this ☐ **c.** those

8. A lot of women died in childbirth in ... days.
- ☐ **a.** these ☐ **b.** those ☐ **c.** the

S'ENTRAÎNER

2 **Complétez cet extrait en utilisant les articles qui conviennent.**

“To Sherlock Holmes she is always *the* woman. I have seldom heard him mention her under any other name. In his eyes she eclipses and predominates the whole of her sex. It was not that he felt any emotion akin to ... love for Irene Adler. All ... emotions, and that one particularly, were abhorrent to his cold, precise but admirably balanced mind. He was, I take it, ... most perfect reasoning and observing machine that ... world has seen, but as ... lover he would have placed himself in ... false position. He never spoke of the softer passions, save with a gibe or sneer. They were ... admirable things for the observer – excellent for drawing the veil from men's motives and actions. But for the trained reasoner to admit such intrusions into his own delicate and finely adjusted temperament was to introduce ... distracting factor which

> seldom: rarement
> akin to: qui ressemble à
> save with a gibe and a sneer: si ce n'était avec quelque moquerie et un sourire méprisant

might throw a doubt upon all his mental results. Grit in a sensitive instrument, or ... crack in one of his own high-power lenses, would not be more disturbing than ... strong emotion in a nature such as his. And yet there was but one woman to him, and that woman was the late Mrs. Adler, of ... dubious and questionable memory.

Sir Arthur Conan Doyle, *A Scandal in Bohemia*, 1888.

grit: ici, un grain de sable
his own high-power lenses: ses puissantes jumelles
the late Mrs Adler: feu Mrs / Madame Adler

3 Complétez les phrases suivantes à l'aide de *this, that, these* ou *those*.

1. ... is the story of a man everybody hates.
2. Which of ... two films would you like to watch?
3. ... will be a good year for wine.
4. She was rich and famous in ... days.
5. Do you remember ... week in Provence? It was a fiasco, wasn't it?
6. At ... time, he was too busy to care.
7. ... time next week I shall be sunbathing in Florida.
8. ... are my books, ... over there are Jenny's.
9. He said he came from a rich family: ... was a lie!
10. Listen to ... : Grandma has a new boyfriend!

SE TESTER

1 1. **c.** Lisa doesn't want to go to **Ø** university next year.
2. **a.** What **Ø** awful weather! It's been raining all day. (*weather* est indénombrable)
3. **a.** **The** painting by Hopper I like best is *Nighthawks.*
4. **b.** They have built **a** hospital on the island.
5. **c.** Mark's brother is in **Ø** jail again.
6. **c.** What? You want to marry **that** stupid woman? You must be mad!
7. **b.** And let me tell you **this**: we shall win!
8. **b.** A lot of women died in childbirth in **those** days.

S'ENTRAÎNER

2 To Sherlock Holmes she is always *the* woman. I have seldom heard him mention her under any other name. In his eyes she eclipses and predominates the whole of her sex. It was not that he felt any emotion akin to **the** love for Irene Adler. All **Ø** emotions, and that one particularly, were abhorrent to his cold, precise but admirably balanced mind. He was, I take it, **the** most perfect reasoning and observing machine that **the** world has seen, but as **a** lover he would have placed himself in **a** false position. He never spoke of the softer passions, save with a gibe or sneer. They were **Ø** admirable things for the observer – excellent for drawing the veil from men's motives and actions. But for the trained reasoner to admit such intrusions into his own delicate and finely adjusted temperament was to introduce **a** distracting factor which might throw a doubt upon all his mental results. Grit in a sensitive instrument, or **a** crack in one of his own high-power lenses, would not be more disturbing than **a** strong emotion in a nature such as his. And yet there was but one woman to him, and that woman was the late Mrs Adler, of **Ø** dubious and questionable memory.

3 1. **This** is the story of a man everybody hates.
2. Which of **these** two films would you like to watch?
3. **This** will be a good year for wine.
4. She was rich and famous in **those** days.
5. Do you remember **that** week in Provence? It was a fiasco, wasn't it?
6. At **that** time, he was too busy to care.
7. **This** time next week I shall be sunbathing in Florida.
8. **These** are my books, **those** over there are Jenny's.
9. He said he came from a rich family: **that** was a lie!
10. Listen to **this**: Grandma has a new boyfriend!

CHAPITRE

12 Les pronoms

Comme son nom l'indique, un pronom sert à remplacer un nom : *Henry / The boy is ambitious, so he works hard.*
Attention au genre et surtout au nombre, car certains noms sont singuliers en anglais : *Kate has beautiful hair. It's thick and shiny.*

I Le choix du pronom personnel

On doit choisir le pronom en fonction de deux critères : le genre et le nombre du référent, c'est-à-dire du nom qu'il remplace.

A Genre

- En général, ***it*** a pour référent un « **inanimé** » (objet, activité, sentiment, idée).

  Of course **love** is important! **It** makes the world go round.
  Bien sûr que c'est important, l'amour. C'est lui qui fait tourner le monde.

- ***It*** renvoie aux **animaux** et aux **bébés** dont on ne connaît pas le sexe ou pour lesquels on n'a pas d'attachement particulier.

  Look at that **dog**! **It**'s huge! And the **baby**! **It**'s so tiny!
  Regarde ce chien ! Il est énorme ! Et le bébé, il est minuscule !

- Les **bateaux** sont souvent repris par ***she***.

  The *Cutty Sark* was destroyed in a fire, wasn't **she**?
  Le *Cutty Sark* a été détruit dans un incendie, je ne me trompe pas ?

B Nombre

- S'accordent au **singulier** :

• ***the USA*** ;

  I just love **the USA. It's** such a cosmopolitan country!
  J'adore les États-Unis. C'est un pays tellement cosmopolite !

• dans la plupart des cas, les noms de **sciences** et **d'activités en *-ics*** : *physics, mathematics, genetics, politics, gymnastics* ;

Mathematics / Maths is fun, isn't **it**?
C'est sympa les maths, non ?

• les **indénombrables**, qui, par définition, n'ont pas de pluriel.

ATTENTION !
Certains mots indénombrables en anglais ont un équivalent français qui, lui, est dénombrable : *advice, furniture, hair, information, luggage, news*, etc. (→ p. 144).
The **news** is good! **It has** never been so good! (news = indénombrable, donc singulier)
Les nouvelles sont bonnes ! Elles n'ont jamais été aussi bonnes !

S'accordent au **pluriel** :

• les **vêtements que l'on enfile par le bas** (pantalon, sous-vêtement, etc.) ;

Heck! My **shorts are** dirty. I must wash **them**.
Zut ! Mon short est sale. Il faut que je le lave.

• les **équipes sportives**.

Arsenal? **They**'re my favourite team!
Arsenal ? C'est l'équipe que je préfère !

Les **noms dits « collectifs »**, parce qu'ils désignent un groupe *(family, government, committee, police)* s'accordent au **singulier** quand on pense au groupe dans son ensemble, et au pluriel si l'on pense plutôt aux individus qui composent ce groupe.

Kate's **family is** / **are** in a state of shock.
La famille de Kate est sous le choc.

The **government** made a mistake. **It** was / **They** were wrong again.
Le gouvernement a commis une erreur. Il s'est encore trompé.

The **police** is worried about the new law. **It**'s very worried indeed.
(*the police* = institution, donc singulier)
La police est inquiète au sujet de la nouvelle loi. Elle est vraiment très inquiète.

The **police** are coming. **They**'re on their way.
(*the police = a group of policemen*, donc pluriel)
La police arrive. / Les policiers arrivent. Ils sont en route.

ATTENTION !

Series : séries(s), feuilleton(s), *species* : espèce(s), *means* : moyen(s) se terminent par un ***s***, même au singulier.

The rhino is **an** endangered **species**. → **it**
Le rhinocéros est une espèce menacée.

A lot of species are threatened by poachers. → **they**
De nombreuses espèces sont menacées par les braconniers.

ZOOM

Pluriels irréguliers à retenir

singulier	pluriel
man • woman	men • women
child	children
mouse	mice
tooth	teeth
wife • knife	wives (épouses) • knives
half • wolf • scarf	halves (moitiés) • wolves • scarves (écharpes)
criterion • phenomenon	criteria (critères) • phenomena
basis • crisis	bases • crises
medium (support, moyen) • curriculum	(the mass) media (les médias) • curricula (programmes scolaires)
syllabus	syllabi / syllabuses (programmes scolaires)
aircraft	aircraft (avions)
sheep	sheep
fish	fish / fishes

II Les pronoms personnels sujets et compléments

pronom sujet	pronom complément
I hate violence.	Does Leo hate **me**?
You're late.	Ada will phone **you**.
She's lovely.	Does mum know **her**?
He loves books.	Zoë likes **him**.
It's dirty.	Tim will clean **it**.
We live here.	Come with **us**!
Will **you** come?	Tom will see **you** all.
They're Spanish.	Dad's met **them**.

ZOOM

Risques d'erreurs

« C'est un(e)… »

C'est une femme formidable. **She**'s a fantastic woman.
C'était un bon joueur de tennis. **He** was a good tennis player.
Les Miller ? Ce sont de vieux amis. The Millers? **They**'re old friends.

« Tim et moi allons à Rome. »

Tim and **I** are going to Rome. (*I* = sujet)

« Moi, je… »

Moi, je pense qu'il est trop tard. *I* think it's too late.

▸ À l'oral, le pronom I sera fortement accentué. À l'écrit, on pourra éventuellement le souligner.

***It* obligatoire**

We found **it** quite difficult to understand him. On a eu du mal à le comprendre.
I like **it** when it snows. J'aime bien quand il neige.

Risques d'erreurs *(suite)*

Traduction de « aussi... que » et « plus... que »

- *as / than* + pronom sujet + verbe (ou auxiliaire)

  She's as funny **as he is.** Elle est aussi drôle que lui.

  He's older **than I am.** Il est plus âgé que moi.

  OU

- *as / than* + pronom complément seul

  She's as funny **as him.** Elle est aussi drôle que lui.

  He's older **than me.** Il est plus âgé que moi.

III Le pronom *one* (pluriel = *ones*)

A *One* remplace un nom dénombrable

"Do you need **a pen**?" "No, thank you, I've got **one**."

(*a pen* = antécédent **dénombrable singulier**, donc ***one***)

« Tu as besoin d'un stylo? » « Non, merci, j'en ai un. »

ATTENTION !

Avec un référent indénombrable, on n'emploie jamais *one*, mais *some*.

"What about **paper**?" "Oh, yes, give me **some**!"

(*paper* = antécédent **indénombrable**, donc *some*)

« Et du papier ? » « Oh, oui, donne-m'en. »

B *The one* et *the ones*

"Look at those girls! **The one** in green looks like a gigantic frog!" (*the one* = celle = **la** fille, singulier)

"Yeah, maybe, but **the** smaller **ones are** cute." (*the ones* = celles = **les** filles, pluriel)

« Regarde un peu ces filles ! Celle qui est en vert ressemble à une grenouille géante ! »
« Peut-être, mais les plus petites sont drôlement mignonnes. »

C *This one* et *that one* (→ p. 117-118)

"Do you want **this** shirt or **that one**?" "**This one**, please."
« Tu veux cette chemise-ci ou celle-là ? » « Celle-ci, s'il te plaît. »

ATTENTION !
Avec un pluriel, ne dites pas ~~*these ones*~~ ni ~~*those ones*~~, mais *these* / *those*.
I like your shoes, especially **these**, but I like **those** you bought in the US too.
J'aime bien tes chaussures, surtout celles-ci, mais j'aime aussi celles que tu as achetées aux États-Unis.

D *Another one* et *the other one(s)*

You've only had one biscuit. Help yourself to **another one**.
Tu n'as pris qu'un seul biscuit. Prends-en un autre.

POUR VOUS AIDER
- Évitez *other ones*. Dites plutôt :
You've only had one biscuit. Help yourself to **some more**.
Tu n'as pris qu'un seul biscuit. Prends-en d'autres.
- En revanche, ***the*** *other one(s)* est tout à fait correct.
We've only seen two museums. Let's see **the other one(s)** now.
Nous n'avons vu que deux musées. Allons voir l'autre / les autres maintenant.

E *One* et le génitif

One complément ne peut apparaître **après un génitif qu'en présence d'un adjectif.**

"Do you like Willa's room?" "I think I prefer Penny's **Ø**."
« Tu aimes la chambre de Willa? » « Je préfère celle de Penny, je crois. »

I prefer my old scooter to Chad's **expensive one**.
Je préfère mon vieux scooter à celui de Chad qui vaut une fortune.

ATTENTION !
~~*The one(s) of*~~ est **incorrect**.
I like Greg's personality but I don't like his sister'**s**. (his sister's personality)
My father's CDs are cool, but I hate my brothers**'**. (my brothers' CDs)

IV Les équivalents du pronom indéfini « on »

A *One* pronom sujet

One sert surtout pour les généralités, les discours moralisateurs, les proverbes. On peut souvent remplacer ***one*** par ***you*** dans ce type de phrases.

One needs love and happiness. On a besoin d'amour et de bonheur.

B *We, you, they*

- Imaginez qu'un Américain parle de son pays, il dira :

  We are very religious in the States. On est très croyants aux États-Unis.

- Si cet Américain parle de la France à un Français :

  Jesus! **You** drive like maniacs here! Bon sang ! On roule comme des dingues dans ce pays !

- S'il parle de l'Allemagne à un Français :

  They drink a lot of beer in Germany. On boit beaucoup de bière en Allemagne.

C La voix passive sans mention de l'agent

The burglar **has been** arrested. **On** a arrêté le cambrioleur.

I was given a book for Christmas. **On** m'a donné un livre pour Noël.

Mais « on » n'est pas toujours la meilleure traduction (→ p. 200).

This carpet was made in Turkey. Ce tapis vient de / a été fabriqué en Turquie.

V Les pronoms réfléchis

singulier	pluriel
I did it **myself**.	**We** did it **ourselves**.
Did **you** enjoy **yourself**?	Did **you** and **Ali** enjoy **yourselves**?
She's just hurt **herself**.	
He's just hurt **himself**.	**They**'ve just hurt **themselves**.
Oh, **that dog**'s just hurt **itself**!	

A *Oneself* : pronom réfléchi indéfini

- On trouve *oneself* dans les définitions des dictionnaires.

  absent oneself (from sth): decide not to be present

- On n'utilise *oneself* que si le sujet est le pronom indéfini ***one***.

  One rarely enjoys **oneself** at funerals. On s'amuse rarement aux enterrements.

- Sinon, n'oubliez pas d'**adapter** ce *oneself*.

  Ada absented **herself**. **Ed and Lea** absented **themselves** too.

ZOOM

Quelques verbes très usités

Verbes avec pronom réfléchi obligatoire	
ask oneself who / why / when / if… brace oneself for : se préparer à enjoy oneself : bien s'amuser	help oneself to : se servir / prendre pride oneself on : s'enorgueillir de take it upon oneself to : prendre sur soi de
Verbes avec pronom réfléchi facultatif	
Behave (yourself)! He identifies (himself) to / with Brad Pitt.	They're preparing (themselves) for trouble!
Verbes réfléchis en français, non réfléchis en anglais	
Hurry up! Dépêche-toi ! I'm bored. Je m'ennuie. Tim washed, shaved and got dressed in five minutes. Tim s'est lavé, rasé et habillé en cinq minutes.	Did you apologize? Tu t'es excusé ? Stop boasting! Arrête de te vanter !

B Les réfléchis emphatiques (d'insistance)

Oliver made the cake **himself**. C'est Oliver (en personne) qui a fait ce gâteau.

C *(All) by oneself*

The little girl stayed at home **(all) by herself**. La petite fille est restée toute seule chez elle.

VI Les pronoms réciproques ⇄

A *Each other* et *one another*

Bill and Ben help **each other / one another** a lot.
Bill et Ben s'entraident beaucoup.

All the guests looked at **each other / one another** and smiled.
Tous les invités se regardèrent et sourirent.

Aujourd'hui, on ne fait plus de distinction entre ***one another*** et ***each other***, bien **plus courant**.

B Absence de pronom récriproque

They are fighting Ø again! [se battre]

They quarrelled Ø about the car. [se quereller]

They argued Ø over / about Leo's choice of career. [se disputer]

VII Les pronoms interrogatifs

questions sur	pronoms interrogatifs correspondants
la nature de qqch. (que, quel)	**What**'s an anagram?
l'identité (qui)	**Who** phoned last night?
le possesseur (à qui)	**Whose** watch is this?
la cause (pourquoi)	**Why** did she say that?
l'époque, le moment (quand)	**When** did it happen?
le lieu (où)	**Where** will you go?
le moyen, la manière (comment)	**How** can I go there?
le choix (lequel, laquelle...)	**Which** CD do you want?
	Which doctor would you like to see?

- Voir aussi les pronoms possessifs (→ p. 136-137) et *own* (→ p. 140).

RÉCAPITULONS

- Le **choix d'un pronom** dépend du genre et du nombre du nom qu'il remplace.
- Les **pronoms réfléchis** reprennent le sujet du verbe.
- Les **pronoms réciproques** soulignent une action exercée par des sujets les uns sur les autres.

SE TESTER QUIZ

1 Choisissez la bonne réponse.

1. The Bradleys are quite poor. I feel really sorry for...
☐ **a.** themselves ☐ **b.** them ☐ **c.** each other ☐ **d.** one another

2. I find ... ridiculous to spend so much money on clothes.
☐ **a.** themselves ☐ **b.** one ☐ **c.** it ☐ **d.** me

3. Perhaps you met her family. ... lived in Madrid in those days.
☐ **a.** They ☐ **b.** She ☐ **c.** Themselves ☐ **d.** One

4. Clara isn't as friendly as ... is.
☐ **a.** he ☐ **b.** him ☐ **c.** himself ☐ **d.** one

5. ... should never drink and drive.
☐ **a.** It ☐ **b.** One ☐ **c.** Oneself ☐ **d.** Yourself

6. I don't like those jeans very much, but the other ... here are really cool.
☐ **a.** one ☐ **b.** ones ☐ **c.** it ☐ **d.** them

7. "What do you think of Matthew's wife?" "She's OK. But I much prefer Sam's ... ."
☐ **a.** one ☐ **b.** ones ☐ **c.** herself ☐ **d.** Ø

8. They helped ... to more fruit juice.
☐ **a.** themselves ☐ **b.** oneself ☐ **c.** ourselves ☐ **d.** it

9. I'm fed up. The children are fighting ... again.
☐ **a.** each other ☐ **b.** Ø ☐ **c.** one another ☐ **d.** themselves

10. Tim and Tom can't work together. They can't stand ... .
☐ **a.** themselves ☐ **b.** them ☐ **c.** oneself ☐ **d.** each other

S'ENTRAÎNER

2 Dites de chacun des mots suivants s'il est singulier, pluriel ou s'il peut être les deux.

trousers	criterion	aerobics	the media	the USA
news	sheep	the police	tights	species

3 Traduisez.

1. C'est une jeune fille au pair adorable. Elle adore nos bébés.
2. Henri VIII ? C'est le roi qui a eu six femmes.
3. Regarde, c'est le *Queen Mary*. C'est un paquebot *(liner)* anglais.
4. Moi, j'aime beaucoup James et Alison. Ce sont de bons amis.
5. Mark et moi avons décidé d'adopter un chien. Nous l'appellerons Sherlock.

SE TESTER

1 1. **b.** The Bradleys are quite poor. I feel really sorry for **them**.

2. **c.** I find **it** ridiculous to spend so much money on clothes.

3. **a.** Perhaps you met her family. **They** lived in Madrid in those days.

4. **a.** Clara isn't as friendly as **he** is.

5. **b.** **One** should never drink and drive.

6. **b.** I don't like those jeans very much, but the other **ones** here are really cool.

7. **d.** "What do you think of Matthew's wife?" "She's OK. But I much prefer Sam's **Ø**."

8. **a.** They helped **themselves** to more fruit juice.

9. **b.** I'm fed up. The children are fighting **Ø** again.

10. **d.** Tim and Tom can't work together. They can't stand **each other**.

S'ENTRAÎNER

2 **Pluriel :** trousers, the media, tights.

Singulier : criterion, aerobics, the USA, news.

Singulier ou pluriel : sheep, the police, species.

3 1. **She** is an adorable au-pair. She loves our bab**ies**.

2. Henry VIII? **He**'s the king who had six **wives**. (*à l'oral* = Henry the eighth)

3. Look! This is the *Queen Mary*. **She** is an English liner.

4. **I** like James and Alison a lot / very much. **They**'re good friends.

5. Mark and **I** have decided to adopt a dog. We'll call **him** Sherlock.

CHAPITRE

13 L'appartenance

Dans *Mandy's garden is lovely*, ou *Mandy's children are funny*, *Mandy* est le « possesseur ». C'est le genre et le nombre du possesseur qui déterminent l'adjectif et le pronom possessif. *Mandy* étant une femme, on dira : *Her garden is lovely. Her children are funny. John* étant un homme, on dira : *John has a lovely garden too, but hers is definitely prettier than his.*

I Whose

A Pronom interrogatif

Whose /hu:z/ sert à identifier le possesseur.

Whose toothbrush is this?
À qui appartient cette brosse à dents ?

B Pronom relatif

Whose marque alors un rapport d'appartenance entre un « possesseur » (animé ou non) et ce qui est « possédé ». Sa traduction la plus courante est « dont ».

The old man **whose** wife is missing is 102! (*the old man* : « possesseur » animé)
Le vieil homme **dont** la femme a disparu a 102 ans !

Animal tests **whose** sole purpose is to make better lipstick should be banned. (*animal tests* : « possesseur » inanimé)
Il faudrait interdire les expériences sur les animaux **dont** le seul but est d'améliorer le rouge à lèvres.

II Les adjectifs possessifs (mon, ma, mes…)

my • *your* • *her* / *his* / *its* • *our* • *your* • *their* + nom(s)

A Particularités de l'anglais

Le choix du possessif de la 3e personne du singulier est déterminé par le **genre du possesseur**.

David's sister → **his** sister

Helen's father → **her** father

the colour of **the door** → **its** colour

B Les parties du corps

En français, elles sont souvent précédées d'un article. En anglais, elles sont souvent précédées d'un adjectif possessif.

He sat there, **his** hands on **his** head.
Il était assis, **les** mains sur **la** tête.

Julia broke **her** nose.
Julia s'est cassé **le** nez.

Mais :

Steve kicked Gary in **the** leg. Gary was kicked in **the** leg.
(Ici, *the leg*, car la jambe n'est pas celle de l'auteur du coup de pied.)

III Les pronoms possessifs (le mien, la mienne…)

mine • *yours* • *hers* / *his* • *ours* • *yours* • *theirs*

A Le choix du pronom possessif

Comme pour les adjectifs possessifs, le choix du pronom possessif dépend uniquement du possesseur.

"Is this your bike?" "Yes, it's **mine**."

"Are these your shoes?" "No, they aren't **mine**."

Your parents are cool. **Mine** are terribly old-fashioned.

B Les pronoms possessifs de la 3e personne du singulier

Comme les adjectifs possessifs, les pronoms possessifs de la 3e personne du singulier sont déterminés par le genre du **possesseur**.

"Is this **Eva's** car?" "Of course, it's **hers**." (Eva → **hers**)
« C'est la voiture d'Eva ? » « Bien sûr (que c'est la sienne). »

"Did those boots belong to **Mr Welsh**?" "Yes, they were **his**." (Mr Welsh → **his**)
« Est-ce que ces bottes appartenaient à Mr Welsh. » « Oui, c'étaient les siennes. »

> **ATTENTION !**
> Il n'y a pas de pronom possessif correspondant à *it*.
> "Is this the cap of your pen?" "Yes." / "Yes, it is." / "Yes, it is the cap of my pen."

C *Of mine, of yours*, etc.

- *A friend of mine* signifie *one of my friends*. C'est une structure très courante.

  Paxton is a friend of yours, isn't he?
  Paxton est un ami à toi, hein ?

- Cette structure peut aussi servir à exprimer divers sentiments.

  Where's that silly little boy of mine? (Ici, affection.)
  Il est où, mon petit bonhomme ?

  Those colleagues of yours make me sick. (Ici, dégoût, colère.)
  Tes collègues me dégoûtent.

IV Le cas possessif (génitif en 's)

A Un seul possesseur

- Lucy Wilson's bag
- the child's clothes
- Thomas's photos /tɒməsɪz/ = Thomas' photos /tɒməs/
  Mr Jones's letter /ˈdʒəʊnzɪz/ = Mr Jones' letter /ˈdʒəʊnz/
- She's a friend of Simon's. (Même structure que *She's a friend of his*.)
  C'est une amie de Simon.

B Plusieurs possesseurs

- *Adrian and Gabriel's toys* : *'s* n'apparaît qu'**une** fois parce que Adrian et Gabriel **partagent** les mêmes jouets.

Hugo's and Justin's toys : *'s* apparaît **deux fois** parce que Hugo et Justin ont **chacun** leurs jouets.

- Les mots au pluriel sont suivis de l'apostrophe uniquement.

the students' results | their parents' anger | the doctors' decision

ATTENTION !
the men's / the women's interests; the children's bags

The Millers' son and the Hills' daughter are in love.
Le fils des Miller et la fille des Hill sont amoureux.

Karen and Mark are friends of my parents'.
(Même structure que *Karen and Mark are friends of theirs*.)
Karen et Mark sont des amis de mes parents.

- Il n'y a pas d'article devant les prénoms *(Ø Harry's secret)*.
- Les noms de famille prennent la marque du pluriel et sont précédés de *the*.

les Jackson : *the Jacksons*

C Emplois du cas possessif

Le cas possessif *('s / ')* est possible avec :

- **les humains**

Edward's salary | the girl's hair
my brothers' jobs | the Brookners' motorbike

- **les animaux**

the cat's green eyes | the dogs' toys

- **les continents, pays, régions, États, villes...**

Asia's economy | the South's plantations | Oxford's libraries

- **les mesures** (temps, distance)

today's paper | next week's agenda
It's only a six miles' drive to the centre of town.
(= It's only a six-mile drive to the centre of town, plus courant).

- **les génitifs de lieu**

  Ava spent two weeks at her dad's. (chez son père)
  I'm going to the Carters'. (chez les Carter)

[Ici, des noms d'habitation (*house, flat*, etc.) sont sous-entendus.]

  I must rush to the baker's (the baker's shop).
  Il faut que je file chez le boulanger / à la boulangerie.

  You should go to the hairdresser's (the hairdresser's salon).
  Tu devrais aller chez le coiffeur.

  We should take Ella to the doctor's (the doctor's surgery).
  On devrait amener Ella chez le médecin.

V Le génitif en *of* (« complément du nom »)

ATTENTION !
Les francophones ont trop souvent recours au génitif en ***'s***.

A *Of* avec les possesseurs humains

Même avec des mots qui font référence à des **humains**, le génitif en *of* peut être préférable au cas possessif (*'s / '*). Parfois même il **s'impose** :

- quand le possesseur est déterminé par plusieurs mots ;

  The arrest of her notoriously violent boyfriend was a relief.
  L'arrestation de son compagnon dont la violence était notoire fut un soulagement.

  He's the son of a rich old Texan businessman.
  C'est le fils d'un vieil et riche homme d'affaires texan.

- quand le possesseur est suivi d'une relative.

  I like the hat of the woman who's talking to Ted.
  J'aime bien le chapeau de la femme qui parle avec Ted.

  The enthusiasm of the students (who are) involved in the scheme is amazing.
  L'enthousiasme des étudiants (qui sont) impliqués dans le projet est incroyable.

B *Of* avec les inanimés

Même si *the painting's colours* ou *the car's alarm* sont tout à fait corrects, choisissez plutôt *of* ; sinon vous risquez, à votre niveau actuel, de produire des énoncés maladroits, voire erronés.

The back of the chair is broken.
Le dossier de la chaise est cassé.

The cruelty of vivisection is obvious.
La cruauté de la vivisection est une évidence.

VI Le génitif « invisible »

Le génitif « invisible », également appelé « génitif elliptique », est ainsi nommé car, bien qu'il y ait un rapport d'appartenance, celui-ci n'est signalé ni par le cas possessif ni par *of*. On le rencontre notamment quand le « possesseur » est la pièce d'une habitation.

The bathroom window is broken.
La fenêtre de la salle de bains est cassée.

My bedroom carpet is yellow.
Le tapis de ma chambre est jaune.

VII *Own*

Toujours employé après un adjectif possessif *(my, your, his...)* ou un cas possessif *(Bert's)*, *own* a souvent un caractère emphatique.

- *Own* peut être **adjectif**.

He has his **own** car.
Il a sa **propre** voiture.

Bert's **own** parents think he's a bit odd.
Même ses propres parents trouvent que Bert est un peu bizarre.

- *Own* peut être **pronom**.

She criticises other people's marriages only to reassure herself that her **own** is OK.
Si elle critique les autres couples, c'est tout simplement pour se rassurer sur l'état du sien.

RÉCAPITULONS

- ***Whose*** est pronom interrogatif ou relatif.
- Quand le possesseur est simple, on a recours au **cas possessif** : *Laura's dog*. Quand il est complexe, on utilise ***of*** : *The father of the boys who crashed into my car has just phoned.*
- En cas de doute, préférez le génitif en *of* au cas possessif.

SE TESTER QUIZ

1 Choisissez la bonne réponse.

1. I wonder ... shoes these are. Could they be Harry's?
☐ **a.** whose ☐ **b.** what ☐ **c.** which

2. The shop ... walls were covered with graffiti belongs to a local politician.
☐ **a.** whose ☐ **b.** its ☐ **c.** her

3. "Is this your car?" "No, it's... ."
☐ **a.** mine ☐ **b.** them ☐ **c.** Helen's

4. "Did they own this land then?" "Yes, it was all ... ."
☐ **a.** people's ☐ **b.** theirs ☐ **c.** hers

5. This hat ... is ridiculous.
☐ **a.** whose ☐ **b.** of yours ☐ **c.** Helen's

6. I've spent two wonderful weeks at ... in Boston.
☐ **a.** my friends ☐ **b.** my friend ☐ **c.** my friends'

7. It's only ... . Don't be so lazy!
☐ **a.** a ten-minute walk ☐ **b.** a ten minutes walk ☐ **c.** a ten minute of walk

S'ENTRAÎNER

2 Traduisez.

1. « À qui est cette moto ? »
« C'est la moto de Gordon. »
2. « Est-ce que c'est ton short ? »
« Non, le mien est rouge. »
3. Emily s'est cassé la jambe hier. Son père est furieux.
4. Les parents de Celia et Tobias marchaient lentement, les mains dans les poches.
5. Janice est une vieille amie de mes parents. Ils se sont rencontrés chez le boucher en 1950.
6. C'est le neveu d'une actrice américaine très célèbre.
7. Tu as le *Times* d'hier ? Mon prof d'histoire a dit qu'il y a un article sur les bibliothèques de Londres.
8. Il veut avoir sa chambre à lui. Il ne veut pas partager *(share)* une petite chambre avec sa chipie de sœur *(silly sister)*.

3 **Complétez avec un adjectif ou un pronom possessif, *whose* ou *of*.**

“[A]ll the women at the dance that night were looking at the young man. It wasn't exactly that he was handsome. There was something else. He was alive in … whole body while the other men walked with great effort and stiffness […] … male bodies had no language of … own in the way that … did. The women themselves seemed confused and lonely in the presence … the young man, and they were ridiculous in … behavior, laughing too loud, blushing like schoolgirls, or casting him a flirting eye. Even the older women were brighter than usual. Mrs Tubby, … face was usually as grim as the statue … General Pickens, the Cherokee hater, played with … necklace until … neck had red lines from the chain. […]
Maybe it was his hands. … hands were strong and dark.
I stayed late, even after wives had pulled … husbands away from … ball game talk and insisted they dance.

Linda Hogan, “*Aunt Moon's Young Man*” in: *Taking Leaves*, 1991.

dance: bal
stiffness: raideur
behavior(u)r: attitude
blushing = becoming red in the face
grim = not happy

SE TESTER

1 **1. a.** I wonder **whose** shoes these are. Could they be Harry's?
2. a. The shop **whose** walls were covered with graffiti belongs to a local politician.
3. c. “Is this your car?” “No, it's **Helen's**.”
4. b. “Did they own this land then?” “Yes, it was all **theirs**.”
5. b. This hat **of yours** is ridiculous.
6. c. I've spent two wonderful weeks at **my friends'** in Boston.
7. a. It's only **a ten-minute walk**. Don't be so lazy!

S'ENTRAÎNER

2 **1.** "**Whose** motorbike is this?"
"It's Gordon**'s**."
2. "Are these **your** shorts?"
"No, **mine** are red." (*shorts* : toujours pluriel)
3. Emily broke **her** leg yesterday. **Her** father is furious.
4. Celia and Tobias**'** / Tobias**'s** parents were walking slowly, **their** hands in **their** pockets.
5. Janice is an old friend **of** my parents**'**. They met at the butcher**'s** in 1950.
6. He's the nephew **of** a very famous American actress.
7. Have you got / Do you have yesterday**'s** *Times*? My history teacher said there's an article about London**'s** libraries.
8. He wants (to have) **his own** (bed)room. He doesn't want to share a small (bed)room with that silly sister **of his**.

3 [A]ll the women at the dance that night were looking at the young man. It wasn't exactly that he was handsome. There was something else. He was alive in **his** whole body while the other men walked with great effort and stiffness. [...] **Their** male bodies had no language of **their** own in the way that **his** did. The women themselves seemed confused and lonely in the presence **of** the young man, and they were ridiculous in **their** behavior, laughing too loud, blushing like schoolgirls, or casting him a flirting eye. Even the older women were brighter than usual. Mrs Tubby, **whose** face was usually as grim as the statue **of** General Pickens, the Cherokee hater, played with **her** necklace until **her** neck had red lines from the chain.[...]
Maybe it was his hands. **His** hands were strong and dark.
I stayed late, even after wives had pulled **their** husbands away from **their** ball game talk and insisted they dance.

CHAPITRE

14 Les quantifieurs

Les quantifieurs permettent d'**évaluer** une quantité. Comme pour les déterminants, leur choix dépend du nom qu'ils accompagnent : dénombrable ou indénombrable.

I Les indénombrables quantifiables

Certains indénombrables peuvent être quantifiés à l'aide d'un partitif (*a piece of, a bit of, a lump of, a drop of*, etc.).

Indénombrables quantifiables	Quantifications
advice : conseil(s)	a word of / a bit of / a piece of advice : un conseil
baggage / luggage : bagage(s)	a suitcase, a bag : un bagage
evidence : preuve(s)	a bit of / a piece of evidence : une preuve
fruit : fruit(s)	a piece of fruit (GB) : un fruit
furniture : meubles	a table, a bed, etc.
homework : les devoirs	a bit of / a piece of homework : un exercice ou une leçon à la maison
gum : chewing-gum	a piece of gum : un chewing-gum
information : renseignement(s)	a piece of information : un renseignement
news : information(s), actualités	a bit of / a piece of news : une nouvelle
sugar : sucre	a lump of sugar : un morceau de sucre
hair : cheveux	a piece of hair : une touffe de cheveux a hair : un cheveu, un poil
transport : transports	a means of transport : un moyen de transport

ATTENTION

- En réalité, *a piece of* est assez rare. Les mots *advice, evidence, information* et *news* sont souvent précédés de *some*, même quand il s'agit d'**un seul** conseil, d'**une seule** preuve, d'**un seul** renseignement, etc.
- Pour *luggage* et *furniture*, on préfère désigner le bagage ou le meuble par le nom qui lui correspond.

II Les indénombrables non quantifiables

A Quelques indénombrables non quantifiables

accomodation : le logement
advertising : la publicité (≠ *an* advertisement : une publicité)
knowledge : la connaissance
leisure : les loisirs
money : l'argent
nonsense : une ineptie / des inepties
permission : l'autorisation
progress : le progrès (an advance, an improvement : un progrès, une amélioration)
rubbish (GB) / garbage (US) : les ordures ménagères / une ânerie / des âneries
trouble : des ennuis
weather : le temps

B *A(n)*

Les indénombrables non quantifiables peuvent toutefois fonctionner avec *a(n)* lorsqu'ils sont précisés par un adjectif ou une relative.

She was overcome by **a** great sadness (**a** great feeling of sadness).
Elle fut envahie d'une grande tristesse.

But she showed **a** courage that everyone admired.
Mais elle montra un courage admiré de tous.

III Les indénombrables « voyageurs »

Certains noms peuvent être indénombrables ou dénombrables, **selon le sens.**

Indénombrables	Dénombrables
Beer is bitter. **Wine** is expensive.	There are famous **beers** in the US. This is **an** excellent **wine.** (un cépage, une appellation)
Good **work**! Bon **travail**.	**a work** by Picasso une **œuvre** de Picasso
She's got blond **hair**. Elle a **les cheveux** blonds.	There was **a hair** on my steak. Il y avait **un cheveu** / **un poil** sur mon steak.
The **damage** was incredible. **Les dégâts** étaient épouvantables.	Sally is claiming **damages**. Sally réclame **des dommages et intérêts**.
Wrap it in **paper**. Enveloppe-le dans du **papier**.	I've bought **a paper**. J'ai acheté **un journal**. We had **a paper** in French. Nous avons eu **un devoir** de français.

IV L'expression de la quantité

A Totalité

Dénombrables singuliers	
tout, tous, tous les...	**whole**: He read the whole book. Il a lu tout le livre.
chaque, les deux, l'un et l'autre	**each**: I've been to New York twice. Each time it was great. **either**: Either car suits me. Les deux voitures me conviennent.
chaque, tous, chacun	**every** (chaque = tous): Every employee must wear a tie. Tous les employés doivent porter une cravate. **each** (chacun, chaque): The manager knows each employee. Le patron connaît chacun des employés.
Dénombrables pluriels	
tout, tous, tous les...	**all**: All three gangsters were arrested.
les deux, l'un et l'autre à la fois	**both**: Both his cats are black. Both Jane and Peter were surprised.
Indénombrables	
tout, tous, tous les...	**all**: Take all the money and all the furniture you can.

B Grande quantité

Dénombrables pluriels	
énormément de	**plenty of, lots of, loads of:** I've got plenty of CDs.
beaucoup de	**a lot of:** He owns a lot of cars. **many:** There are many tourists here.
pas mal de	**quite a lot of:** Quite a lot of flights were cancelled. Pas mal de vols ont été annulés. **quite a few:** Quite a few students complained. Pas mal d'étudiants se sont plaints.
Indénombrables	
énormément de	**plenty of, lots of, loads of:** I've got loads of work to do. **a great deal of:** It takes a great deal of patience to do that.
beaucoup de	**a lot of:** I've got a lot of time. **much:** He had much trouble with his sister.
pas mal de	**quite a lot of:** It took quite a lot of courage. Il a fallu pas mal de courage.

C Quantité excessive, suffisante et insuffisante

Dénombrables pluriels	
trop de	**too many:** There are too many cars.
assez de	**enough:** He has enough toys.
pas assez de	**not enough:** There aren't enough chairs. **too few / only a few:** Too few students / Only a few students passed the exam. Trop peu d'étudiants / Seuls quelques étudiants ont réussi l'examen.
Indénombrables	
trop de	**too much:** You're making too much noise!
assez de	**enough:** I've got enough food.
pas assez de	**not enough:** I don't have enough money. **too little:** We've got too little time.

D Petite quantité

Dénombrables pluriels	
quelques	a few: A few spectators showed up. Quelques spectateurs sont venus.
peu de	few: I've got very few books. J'ai très peu de livres.
Indénombrables	
quelques, un peu de	a little: I need a little advice and a little money. J'ai besoin de quelques conseils et d'un peu d'argent.
peu de	little: I have very little patience. J'ai très peu de patience.

E Quantité indéterminée (non précisée)

Dénombrables pluriels	
plusieurs	several: I wrote several letters. J'ai écrit plusieurs lettres.
du, de la, des	some: Some dogs are very clever. any: Are there any crisps? Y a-t-il des chips ?
Indénombrables	
du, de la, des	some: Could I have some sugar, please? I'd like some coffee, please. any: Is there any coffee left? Est-qu'il reste du café ?

SOME OU ANY ?

- On utilise *some* dans les questions pour lesquelles on attend (ou on fait semblant d'attendre) une réponse positive.
"Would you like some coffee?"

- *Any* a une coloration neutre ou négative. On l'utilise notamment quand on ignore si la réponse sera « oui » ou « non ».
"Are there any biscuits, Dad?"

- *Any* signifie aussi « n'importe quel(s) / quelle(s) », sous-entendu « peu importe ».
Any candle will do. N'importe quelle bougie fera l'affaire.

F Quantité quasiment nulle ou nulle

Dénombrables singuliers	
pas de / aucun	**no**: I've no idea where he is.
Dénombrables pluriels	
pas de / aucun	**not any**: They haven't got any chairs. **no**: She had no shoes on! **none of**: None of them has / have a pen! **neither of**: Neither of the children want(s) to go to bed. Aucun des (deux) enfants ne veut aller se coucher.
presque pas de	**hardly any, barely any**: There were hardly any children. Il n'y avait presque pas d'enfants.
Indénombrables	
pas de / aucun	**not any**: There isn't any bread left. **no**: He felt no remorse. Il n'éprouvait aucun remord.
presque pas de	**hardly any, barely any**: There's hardly any tea left. Il ne reste presque plus de thé.

NONE* ET *NEITHER

- *None* s'emploie quand il y a au moins trois éléments.
- *Neither* est toujours associé à deux éléments.

RÉCAPITULONS

- Avant de choisir un quantifieur, assurez-vous que vous savez bien à quelle catégorie (dénombrable / indénombrable) appartient le nom qu'il accompagne. Vérifiez dans un dictionnaire si nécessaire.
- Attention : certains noms dénombrables en français sont indénombrables en anglais (*advice, news, information*, etc.).

SE TESTER QUIZ

1 Choisissez la bonne proposition.

1. "Which hat do you prefer? The green one or the yellow one?" "I like them ... ."
☐ **a.** either ☐ **b.** both ☐ **c.** each ☐ **d.** every

2. ... child was given a small dictionary.
☐ **a.** Each ☐ **b.** Both ☐ **c.** Whole ☐ **d.** All

3. She spent the ... day working for her exam.
☐ **a.** all ☐ **b.** every ☐ **c.** whole ☐ **d.** each

4. Greg says he does not need ... help.
☐ **a.** several ☐ **b.** any ☐ **c.** a little ☐ **d.** some

5. It is a very difficult book. That's why very ... people have read it.
☐ **a.** little ☐ **b.** some ☐ **c.** few ☐ **d.** a few

6. "Are there ... messages?" "... , I'm afraid."
☐ **a.** little / Some ☐ **b.** some / Few ☐ **c.** any / None

S'ENTRAÎNER

2 Complétez les phrases suivantes à l'aide de quantifieurs exprimant :

1. la totalité

a. Listen you two. .... of you should be back by 10.
b. You can take .... road. .... lead to Pertenhall.
c. Have you been working .... day? You look tired.
d. She wants to bequeath *(léguer)* her .... fortune to the Conservative Party.
e. There are shops on .... side of the avenue.
f. I must go to school .... day. What a drag *(quelle barbe)*!
g. .... house had a different colour. It was simply amazing!
h. .... team *(équipe)* was good. It was a very boring football match.

2. une grande quantité

a. Too .... people spend too .... money on clothes.
b. .... people were shocked and complained.
c. It takes .... courage to admit you are wrong.
d. I didn't think you would have so .... luck!
e. Quite .... paintings were stolen last night.

3. une quantité excessive, suffisante ou insuffisante

a. There are still too .... women in politics.
b. Too .... things to do and too .... time!
c. It's getting cooler at this time of year. Do you have .... blankets *(couvertures)*?
d. Too .... sleep is bad for you. You should go to bed earlier.
e. "How much money do you have?" "Very .... , I'm afraid."

4. une petite quantité

a. .... sportsmen succeed without practising a lot.
b. Unfortunately, there's less snow than last year, that's why there are .... tourists.
c. Could you give me .... sugar, please?
d. You have to give .... of your time if you really want to help.

5. une quantité indéterminée

a. Have .... caviar, it's delicious!
b. I own .... pairs of roller skates, but .... of them are badly damaged.
c. Can you lend me .... CDs, please?
d. Did the burglar leave .... fingerprints on the desk?

6. une quantité nulle ou presque nulle

a. I'm fed up with you all. .... of you ever helps me!
b. "Did they ask many questions?" "No, ... in fact."
c. Sorry, I can't give you .... advice, I'm afraid.
d. I was listening for some noise, but there was ....
e. He was disappointed. .... celebrities showed up *(se montrer)* at his party.
f. I've hardly got .... friends here.

3 Traduisez les phrases suivantes.

1. Il ne m'a pas donné beaucoup de conseils.
2. Il n'y a pas assez de preuves contre eux.
3. Ses cheveux étaient blonds et sales.
4. Les informations qu'ils nous ont données ont été très utiles.
5. Ces meubles ont été achetés dans un marché aux puces *(a flea market)* de Londres.
6. N'importe quel hôtel fera l'affaire *(will do)*. Je ne suis pas difficile *(fussy)*.

SE TESTER

1 1. **b.** "Which hat do you prefer? The green one or the yellow one?" "I like them **both**."
2. **a. Each** child was given a small dictionary.
3. **c.** She spent the **whole** day working for her exam.
4. **b.** Greg says he does not need **any** help.
5. **c.** It is a very difficult book. That's why very **few** people have read it.
6. **c.** "Are there **any** messages?" "**None**, I'm afraid."

S'ENTRAÎNER

2 1. **a.** Listen you two. **Both** of you should be back by 10.
b. You can take **either** road. **Both** lead to Pertenhall.
c. Have you been working **all** day? You look tired.
d. She wants to bequeath her **whole** fortune to the Conservative Party.
e. There are shops on **either** side of the avenue.
f. I must go to school **every / each** day. What a drag!
g. Each house had a different colour. It was simply amazing!
h. Neither team was good. It was a very boring football match.

2. **a.** Too **many** people spend too **much** money on clothes.
b. A lot of / Lots of / Many / Quite a few people were shocked and complained.
c. It takes **a great deal / a lot of** courage to admit you are wrong.
d. I didn't think you would have so **much** luck!
e. Quite **a lot of / a few** paintings were stolen last night.

3. **a.** There are still too **few** women in politics.
b. Too **many** things to do and too **little** time!
c. It's getting cooler at this time of year. Do you have **enough** blankets?
d. Too **little** sleep is bad for you. You should go to bed earlier.
e. "How much money do you have?" "Very **little**, I'm afraid."

4. **a. Few** sportsmen succeed without practising a lot.
b. Unfortunately, there's less snow than last year, that's why there are **few / fewer** tourists.
c. Could you give me **a little** sugar, please?
d. You have to give **a little** of your time if you really want to help.

5. **a.** Have **some** caviar, it's delicious!
b. I own **several** pairs of roller skates, but **some** of them are badly damaged.
c. Can you lend me **some** CDs, please?
d. Did the burglar leave **any** fingerprints on the desk?

6. **a.** I'm fed up with you all. **None** of you ever helps me!
b. "Did they ask many questions?" "No, **none / hardly any** in fact."
c. Sorry, I can't give you **any** advice, I'm afraid.
d. I was listening for some noise, but there was **none**.
e. He was disappointed. **No** celebrities showed up at his party.
f. I've hardly got **any** friends here.

3 1. He didn't give me **much advice**.
2. There isn't **enough** evidence against them.
3. His / Her **hair was** blond and dirty.
4. The **information** they gave us **was** most useful.
5. **This furniture was** bought at a London flea market.
6. **Any** hotel will do. I'm not fussy.

CHAPITRE

15 Les adjectifs qualificatifs

L'adjectif qualificatif est invariable en anglais : *Mandy is adorable. Sarah and Max are adorable too.* Comme en français, il peut être épithète : *a small house* ou attribut : *The house is small.*

I L'ordre des adjectifs épithètes

- En anglais, les adjectifs **épithètes** se trouvent **toujours devant** le(s) nom(s) qu'ils qualifient.

  Emily wants a black jacket. Emily veut une veste noire.

- Quand **deux** adjectifs se suivent, l'adjectif qui désigne la caractéristique la plus durable ou la plus objective se place **juste devant** le mot qualifié.

  Jason is a handsome tall guy. [*Tall* est plus objectif que *handsome* (beau).]

- Quand **trois** adjectifs (ou plus) se suivent, l'ordre est le suivant :

1. opinion *(beautiful, silly...)*
2. taille ou dimension *(long, short...)*
3. âge ou époque *(old, eighteenth-century...)*
4. forme *(square, round...)*
5. couleur *(green...)*
6. origine ou nationalité *(Italian, Spanish...)*
7. matière *(wood, metal...)*

Contentez-vous de groupes de deux, au maximum trois adjectifs.
Alberta was an **ugly** (1) **fat** (2) woman. Alberta était une grosse femme laide.
Jason's got **gorgeous** (1) **big** (2) **blue** (5) eyes. Jason a de grands yeux bleus magnifiques.
She had **short** (2) **straight** (4) **brown** (5) hair. Elle avait les cheveux bruns, courts et raides.

II Les adjectifs composés

Retenez ceux que vous rencontrez, mais **évitez d'en créer vous-même**.

A Construction

Adjectif + nom + *ed*

broad (large) + mind (esprit) → a broad-minded mother : une mère tolérante

short (court) + sight (vue) → a short-sighted girl : une fille myope

AUTRES ADJECTIFS À CONNAÎTRE

a **narrow-minded** politician: un homme politique à l'esprit étroit

a **blue-eyed** baby: un bébé aux yeux bleus

a **red-haired** boy: un garçon aux cheveux roux

Adverbe + participe passé

carefully + made → a carefully-made decision : une décision mûrement réfléchie

beautifully + written → a beautifully-written novel : un roman joliment écrit

Nom + participe passé ou nom + V-*ing*

home + made → a home-made cake : un gâteau fait maison

time + (to) consume → a time-consuming job : un métier (très) prenant

Adjectif + V-*ing*

fast + (to) change → English is a fast-changing language. L'anglais est une langue qui évolue à toute vitesse.

good + (to) look → Elena is very good-looking. Elena est très jolie.

AUTRES ADJECTIFS À CONNAÎTRE

a **hard-working** student: un élève / un étudiant travailleur

a **healthy-looking** child: un enfant qui a l'air d'être en bonne santé

Autres structures possibles

- Nom + nom : a **soundproof** studio (un studio insonorisé)
- Nom + adjectif : an **alcohol-free** drink (une boisson sans alcool)
- Adverbe + adjectif : an **environmentally-friendly** measure (une mesure écologique)
- Nom + adjectif : an **ozone-friendly** spray (un aérosol qui respecte la couche d'ozone)

B L'expression de la mesure

La distance, la taille, le poids, la durée et l'âge peuvent être exprimés par un adjectif dont le schéma est le suivant : **nombre + unité** (distance, taille, poids, durée, âge) **au singulier** (→ p. 139).

It was a two-mile walk to the village. Il fallait faire trois kilomètres à pied pour aller au village.

We bought a six-pound pumpkin. Nous avons acheté un potiron de trois kilos.

It's a three-hour drive to Cape Cod. Il faut trois heures de voiture pour aller à Cape Cod.

She teaches five-year-old children. Elle enseigne à des élèves de cinq ans.

III Les adjectifs substantivés

Un adjectif substantivé (nominalisé) est un adjectif transformé en nom.

A Sans marque du pluriel

the rich (les riches)

the poor (les pauvres)

the young (les jeunes)

the elderly (les personnes âgées)

the blind (les aveugles)

the deaf (les sourds)

the disabled (les handicapés)

ATTENTION

Au singulier, la présence d'un nom est obligatoire : a rich man, a middle-aged woman, a poor girl.

B Avec marque du pluriel

- The Whites, the Americans, the Italians, the Asians, etc.

POUR VOUS AIDER

- Notez bien la majuscule.
- Il n'y a pas de s aux mots en ch et sh : the French, the Dutch (les Néerlandais), the Irish (les Irlandais). Au singulier, on dira a Frenchman (en un mot), a French woman, a French boy.

- The Catholics, the Protestants, the Evangelicals, the Muslims (les musulmans), the Jews (les juifs), etc.
- The Republicans, the Liberals, the Conservatives, the Socialists, the Greens, etc.
- The grown-ups (les adultes), the twenty-year-olds (les personnes de vingt ans).

IV Les adjectifs suivis d'une préposition

about	crazy / mad about (fou de), upset about (contrarié par), concerned / worried about (inquiet pour), be right / wrong about (avoir raison / tort au sujet de)
at	mad at (furieux contre), good / excellent / brilliant at (bon / excellent / brillant en), bad / hopeless at (mauvais / nul en)
for	responsible for (responsable de)
from	different from (différent de)
in	be interested in (s'intéresser à / être intéressé par), disappointed in sb (déçu par qqn)
on	be keen on (aimer : I'm keen on swimming.)
of	be fond of (aimer : He's very fond of Leila.)
to	new to (nouveau pour), superior / inferior to
with	be fed up with (en avoir assez de : I'm fed up with school.), be disappointed with sth (être déçu par qqch.)

V Les comparatifs

A Les comparatifs de supériorité

- Adjectifs courts *(big, fat, fit, tall, long, slow...)* → adjectif + *er (+ than)*

  Emma is taller than her mother.

- Adjectifs longs : *more* + adjectif *(+ than)*

  Mr Woods is more eccentric than Mr Bell.

MODIFICATIONS ORTHOGRAPHIQUES

- Big, fat, fit : voyelle brève suivie d'une seule consonne → bigger, fatter, fitter.
- Adjectifs de deux syllabes en y : funny → funnier.

Bob is funnier than you.

FORMES IRRÉGULIÈRES

- *good* → *better (than)*

Her first film was excellent, but this one is even better.
Son premier film était excellent, mais celui-ci est encore meilleur.

- *bad* → *worse* (pire)

It's awful! My results are even worse than yours!
C'est affreux ! Mes résultats sont encore pires / plus mauvais que les tiens !

- *far* (loin) → *farther* (plus loin)

Rome is farther than Florence. Rome est plus loin que Florence.

- *further* (supplémentaire)

I need further information. J'ai besoin de plus de renseignements.

B Les comparatifs d'infériorité

- ***Less* + adjectif + *than***, quel que soit l'adjectif.

Lola is **less** indifferent **than** Nick. Lola est moins indifférente que Nick.

- Avec les adjectifs d'une seule syllabe, on emploie très souvent ***not so* + adjectif + *as***.

John is **not so** big **as** Peter. John est moins costaud que Peter.

ATTENTION

Ne confondez pas *not so good as* (moins bon / moins bien que) et *worse than* (pire que).

This film is not so good as her first.
Ce film est moins réussi que son premier.

She's worse than him.
Elle est pire que lui.

C Les comparatifs d'égalité

As + **adjectif** + *as*, quel que soit l'adjectif.

He was **as** lazy **as** his sister. Il était aussi paresseux que sa sœur.

VI Les superlatifs

A Les superlatifs de supériorité

- Adjectifs courts: *the* + adjectif + *-est*

slow → This is **the slowest** train in England. C'est le train le plus lent de toute l'Angleterre.

fat → She's **the fattest** woman I know. C'est la femme la plus grosse que je connaisse.

- Adjectifs longs : *the most* + adjectif

She is the most attractive girl I've ever seen.

MODIFICATIONS ORTHOGRAPHIQUES

- Comme pour les comparatifs, on double la consonne finale après une voyelle brève : the fattest, the biggest, etc.
- Adjectifs de deux syllabes en *y* : funny → the funniest.

FORMES IRRÉGULIÈRES

- *good* → *the best*

This is definitely his best book. C'est vraiment son meilleur livre.

- *bad* → *the worst* (le pire)

It's the worst concert I've ever been to. C'est le plus mauvais concert que j'aie jamais vu.

- *far* (loin) → *the farthest*

What is the farthest planet? Quelle est la planète la plus éloignée ?

THE LAST, THE LATEST

- *(the) last* : le dernier (il n'y en aura pas d'autre) ≠ *(the) latest* : le dernier en date (il y en aura d'autres)

He wrote his last book in 1890. Il a écrit son dernier livre en 1890.

Have you bought her latest CD yet?
Est-ce que tu as (déjà) acheté son (tout) dernier CD ?

B Les superlatifs d'infériorité : *the least* + adjectif

He was the least competent doctor. C'était le médecin le moins compétent.

ATTENTION
The least est très rare avec les adjectifs courts. On ne dit pas ~~the least tall girl~~, mais the smallest girl.

C Le superlatif avec deux éléments

En anglais britannique, quand deux éléments sont comparés (le plus / le moins sympathique des deux frères), l'adjectif a la forme d'un comparatif, et non d'un superlatif.

En anglais américain, on a la forme du superlatif quel que soit le nombre d'éléments.

It was the more interesting story (of the two). (US : the most interesting)
Des deux histoires, c'était la plus intéressante

She is the less beautiful of the two sisters. (US : the least beautiful)
C'est la moins belle des deux sœurs.

D Le superlatif avec *of* ou *in* ?

- Superlatif avec un groupe, un nombre ou une période : ***of***

He's the cleverest **of** them all. C'est le plus malin de tous.

It was the worst day **of** the week.

- Superlatif avec un lieu : ***in***

The kitchen is the smallest room **in** the flat.

VII Progression et évolution proportionnelle

A Progression (« de plus en plus », « de moins en moins »)

She is getting **more and more** arrogant. Elle devient de plus en plus arrogante.

They are becoming **less and less** sociable. Ils sont de moins en moins sociables.

B Évolution proportionnelle (« plus…, plus… » ; « moins…, moins… »)

The more I love you, **the more** I need you. Plus je t'aime, (et) plus j'ai besoin de toi.

The sooner, **the better**. Le plus tôt sera le mieux.

The less I work, **the less** I want to work. Moins je travaille, (et) moins j'ai envie de travailler.

RÉCAPITULONS

- L'adjectif est invariable.
- Épithète, il précède le nom.
- Ne confondez pas comparatifs (*taller than, more interesting than*) et superlatifs (*the tallest, the most interesting*).

SE TESTER QUIZ

1 Choisissez la bonne solution.

1. Who will win the next election? That is ... question, isn't it?
❑ **a.** a thousand dollar ❑ **b.** a thousand dollars ❑ **c.** a thousand-dollar

2. He wore a ... suit.
❑ **a.** blue Italian beautiful ❑ **b.** beautiful blue Italian
❑ **c.** Italian beautiful blue

3. Have you been dieting, Simon? You look much ... !
❑ **a.** the thinnest ❑ **b.** thinnest ❑ **c.** thinner

4. You can travel by train or fly, but the train is ... , of course.
❑ **a.** cheaper ❑ **b.** cheapest ❑ **c.** the cheapest

5. It's ... than a car but ... !
❑ **a.** fastest / noiser ❑ **b.** faster / noisiest ❑ **c.** faster / noisier

6. That was ... boring film I had ever seen!
❑ **a.** the most ❑ **b.** more ❑ **c.** the more

7. ... I see them, ... !
❑ **a.** The more / the best ❑ **b.** The less / the worst ❑ **c.** The less / the better

S'ENTRAÎNER

2 Intégrez dans le bon ordre les adjectifs proposés entre parenthèses.

1. Jude is the .... boy who is in Sam's class. (American / little)
2. Mr Parks is the .... man next-door. (silly / old)
3. Sara is the .... girl sitting next to Orlando. (German / red-haired / tiny)
4. She bought a pair of .... earrings. (red / triangular)
5. I'll buy a .... carpet. (huge / blue / rectangular)
6. Emma has .... eyes. (big / lovely / brown)
7. When I first met Tasha, she had .... hair. (auburn / curly / long)
8. Miranda wore a .... dress. (short / English / green)

tiny: minuscule
curly: bouclés

3 **Complétez en choisissant parmi les adjectifs présentés pages 155-156.**

1. Don't drink this! It's not .... ! You don't want to get drunk, do you?
2. If we leave at nine, we'll get there for lunch. It's only a ...... drive to Chester.
3. You say it's a ...... walk to the beach. That's a bit far. I'll take a bus.
4. This ...... marmalade is delicious. It's much better than the marmalade you buy from the supermarket.
5. What a ...... letter! Rod will become a famous writer I'm sure.
6. Mind you, the sixth child was not an accident, but a ...... decision.
7. Matilda is extremely .... She could become a model.
8. I think you're .... You should wear glasses.
9. Mum and Dad are furious because Alex is going out with an older girl. They're so ...... !
10. When I met him, in 2007, he had a ...... daughter. She was born in the US, in 2002.

4 **Toutes ces phrases sont absurdes. Corrigez-les en utilisant un comparatif de supériorité comme dans l'exemple.**

London is smaller than Paris. → London is (much) bigger than Paris.

1. The Seine is larger than the Mississippi River.
2. Jenifer Lopez is older than Madonna.
3. Los Angeles is an older city than New York.
4. Tom Cruise is taller than Joakim Noah.
5. The Château de Versailles is smaller than the White House.
6. Kate Moss is fatter than most women.
7. Pluto is closer to the sun than the moon is.
8. Gold is lighter than paper.
9. A classroom is quieter than an empty church.
10. A car is slower than a bike.

5 On vous donne la réponse. Imaginez la question : elle devra comprendre l'adjectif donné entre parenthèses et, selon les cas, un superlatif de supériorité ou d'infériorité.

New York City (cosmopolitan) → What is the most cosmopolitan city in the United States?

1. The USA. (powerful)
2. China. (populated)
3. Sam, of course! He's gorgeous. His brother is not so handsome. (good-looking)
4. My English teacher. He's great. (competent)
5. Mr James. He's such a boring teacher! (bad)
6. I can't remember the title. But it was a very bad novel. (interesting)
7. The twins, Leo and Lea were born yesterday. They're very small. Leo. (tiny)
8. *The Night of the Hunter*, by Charles Laughton. You should buy the DVD! (good)
9. The blue T-shirt. I only paid £2 for it. The green one cost me £7. (expensive)
10. Miss Parker. She earns £30,000 a year. The other secretaries earn less. (well-paid).

SE TESTER

1 1. **c.** Who will win the next election? That is **a thousand-dollar** question, isn't it?
2. **b.** He wore a **beautiful blue Italian** suit.
3. **c.** Have you been dieting, Simon? You look much **thinner**!
4. **a.** You can travel by train or fly, but the train is **cheaper**, of course!
5. **c.** It's **faster** than a car but **noisier**.
6. **a.** That was **the most** boring film I had ever seen!
7. **c.** **The less** I see them, **the better**!

S'ENTRAÎNER

2 1. the little American boy 2. the silly old man 3. the tiny red-haired German girl 4. triangular red earrings 5. a huge rectangular blue carpet 6. lovely big brown eyes 7. long curly auburn hair 8. a short green English dress

3 1. alcohol-free 2. three-hour 3. two-mile 4. home-made 5. beautifully-written 6. carefully-made 7. good-looking 8. short-sighted 9. narrow-minded 10. five-year-old

4 **1.** The Seine is smaller than the Mississippi River.
2. Jenifer Lopez is younger than Madonna.
3. Los Angeles is a more recent city than New York.
4. Tom Cruise is (much) smaller than Joakim Noah.
5. The Château de Versailles is bigger / larger than the White House.
6. Kate Moss is (much) thinner than most women.
7. Pluto is **farther from** the sun than the moon is.
8. Gold is (much) heavier than paper.
9. A classroom is more noisy / noisier than an empty church.
10. A car is faster than a bike.

5 **1.** What is the most powerful country in the world?
2. What is the most populated country in Asia / in the world?
3. Which is the better-looking of the two brothers? (US: the best-looking, ➜ p. 160)
4. Who / Which is your most competent teacher? / Which of your teachers is the most competent (of all)?
5. Who / Which is your worst teacher? / Which of your teachers is the worst?
6. What's the least interesting book you've (ever) read?
7. Which is the tinier of the two? (US: the tiniest, ➜ p. 160)
8. What's the best film you've (ever) seen?
9. Which (T-shirt / of the two T-shirts) was the less expensive? (US: the least expensive, ➜ p. 160)
10. Who / Which is the best-paid secretary?

CHAPITRE

16 Les adverbes

Les adverbes permettent de préciser une action : *She walked slowly*, un adjectif : *He's seriously ill*, ou d'autres adverbes : *She speaks incredibly well*.

I Les adverbes de manière

A Formation

En général, ils se forment en ajoutant *-ly* à l'adjectif. Attention à certaines modifications orthographiques.

adjectif	adverbe	adjectif	adverbe
mad	madly	irresponsible	irresponsi**bly** (sans e)
final	finally	true	tru**ly** (sans e)
fortunate	fortunately	dramatic	dramatic**ally**
desperate	desperately	specific	specific**ally**
possible	possi**bly** (sans e)	happy	happ**ily** (y → i)

B Faux-amis

actually : vraiment, réellement	actuellement : now / currently
eventually : au bout du compte / finalement	éventuellement : possibly
lately : récemment	tard : late

***BADLY* : MAL / BEAUCOUP / VRAIMENT**

They treat him badly. Ils le traitent mal.

I miss you badly, darling. Tu me manques beaucoup, mon amour.

Your hair is too long, you badly need a cut. Tes cheveux sont trop longs. Il faut vraiment que tu les fasses couper.

C *Good* et *well*

adjectif	adverbe
She's a good dancer.	She dances well.
She's a better dancer than me.	She dances better than me.
	She's the one who dances [the] best.

D *Hard, fast, late, early, daily, weekly, monthly, yearly*

Ces mots sont tantôt adverbes, tantôt adjectifs.

adjectif	adverbe
She loves fast cars.	Don't drive so fast!
He was late, as usual.	We arrived late.
I like my daily routine. J'aime bien mon train-train quotidien.	He writes daily. Il écrit tous les jours.

E Les adjectifs en *-ly*

Malgré leur terminaison en *-ly*, ***lonely, lovely, silly, friendly*** sont des adjectifs. Pour exprimer la manière, on dira :

He's a silly man. He always acts in a silly manner.
Il est bête. Il se comporte toujours bêtement.

QUELQUES ADVERBES DE MANIÈRE

nicely ≠ nastily, unpleasantly, horribly • honestly ≠ dishonestly • generously ≠ selfishly • tactfully ≠ tactlessly • peacefully ≠ aggressively, violently • politely ≠ impolitely, rudely • interestingly ≠ uninterestingly • modestly ≠ vainly • patiently ≠ impatiently • respectfully ≠ disrespectfully

II Les adverbes de temps

A Moment

Les principaux adverbes sont : *now, today, yesterday, tomorrow, soon, late.*

B Chronologie

- *first(ly) / first of all* : d'abord / pour commencer / tout d'abord
- *then / next / afterwards / subsequently / later* : puis / ensuite / plus tard
- *meanwhile / in the meantime* : en attendant
- *finally / eventually / in the end / last / lastly* : finalement / pour terminer

> *At last* permet d'exprimer un soulagement ou la colère.
> Here you are at last! Ah, enfin, tu arrives ! (Ce n'est pas trop tôt.)

C Fréquence

- Les principaux adverbes sont : *always, often, frequently, sometimes, occasionally, rarely, hardly ever, never.*

- *Never* et *hardly ever* sont accompagnés d'un verbe à la forme affirmative.

  I never smoke. Je ne fume jamais.
  He hardly ever cries. Il ne pleure presque jamais.

- *Hardly* seul signifie « pratiquement pas » / « à peine » / « très peu ».

  I can hardly hear a word he says. Je n'entends pratiquement pas ce qu'il dit.

D Place des adverbes de fréquence

- Attention surtout à ***often*** qui obéit à des règles strictes. Il se place :
  - après *be* : He **is often** sick.
  - avant le verbe *have* : He **often has** too much work.
  - avec le présent et le prétérit simples des autres verbes : She **often went** to Cork. / She **went** to Cork **often**.
  - entre l'auxiliaire *have* et le verbe : I **have often seen** them.

- Les autres adverbes sont plus mobiles.

  Sometimes, we had a little chat. / We had a little chat sometimes. / We sometimes had a little chat. Parfois, nous bavardions un peu.

Tous les combien ≠ combien de fois

- Interrogation sur la **fréquence**

How **often** do you see her? Tu la vois tous les combien ?

- Interrogation sur le **nombre de fois**

How many times have you seen her? Combien de fois l'as-tu vue ?

III Les équivalents de « encore »

Si « encore » signifie « de nouveau » : *again*

She's in jail **again**. Elle est de nouveau en prison.

Si « encore » signifie que rien n'a changé : *still*

Lisa isn't here. She's **still** in Texas. Lisa n'est pas là. Elle est encore / toujours au Texas.

Quand l'action n'est toujours pas accomplie (« pas encore ») : *not yet*

- Question

Has he gone **yet**? Est-ce qu'il est déjà parti ?

- Réponse négative (pas encore)

No, **not yet**. / No, he has**n't** gone **yet**. / No, he hasn't.

IV *Enough* /ɪ'nʌf/

Adjectif / adverbe + *enough*

This box isn't big **enough**. Cette boîte n'est pas assez grande.

She doesn't swim fast **enough**. Elle ne nage pas assez vite.

***Enough* + nom**

I'll have **enough** money.

RÉCAPITULONS

- La place de l'adverbe change en fonction de sa **nature** (adverbe de fréquence et adverbe de temps par exemple).
- *Enough* se place toujours **après un adjectif** et toujours **devant un nom**.
- Retenez bien les adverbes *well, fast* et *hard*.

SE TESTER QUIZ

1 Choisissez la bonne réponse.

1. They ... in that small restaurant downtown.
☐ **a.** had often dinner ☐ **b.** often had dinner ☐ **c.** had dinner often

2. Ken isn't ... to leave Barbie. Besides, he doesn't have ... to live on his own.
☐ **a.** enough brave / money enough ☐ **b.** brave enough / enough money
☐ **c.** enough brave / enough money

3. "... do you go to the gym?" "Twice a week."
☐ **a.** How many times ☐ **b.** How often ☐ **c.** How long

4. Mrs. Parks is a wonderful patient: she ... complains.
☐ **a.** still ☐ **b.** again ☐ **c.** hardly ever

5. Two o'clock in the afternoon and he's ... in bed!
☐ **a.** again ☐ **b.** still ☐ **c.** yet

6. "Has he taken his flight ... ?" "No, he's ... waiting at the airport."
☐ **a.** yet / still ☐ **b.** still / not yet ☐ **c.** yet / not yet

S'ENTRAÎNER

2 Formez l'adverbe qui correspond à l'adjectif proposé.

1. sad 2. full 3. desperate 4. unfortunate 5. admirable 6. fashionable 7. final 8. drastic 9. lucky 10. seeming *(apparent)*

3 Traduisez ces phrases. Les mots en gras doivent être traduits par un adverbe.

1. « Qu'est-ce qu'il a dit **en réalité** ? »
« Il a dit que l'appartement n'était pas **assez** confortable. »
2. Après avoir vu le médecin, il a **finalement** décidé de faire un régime *(go on a diet)*.
3. Je suis épuisé. J'ai **impérativement** besoin de vacances *(a holiday)*.
4. Est-ce que tu as vu une bonne pièce de théâtre *(a play)* **récemment** ?
5. Lisa travaille **bien**. Elle travaille encore **mieux** que son chef.
6. Je me suis couché **tard** hier *(last night)*. Je travaille **dur** parce que j'ai *(take)* mes examens la semaine prochaine.
7. Laisse Sophie dormir et **en attendant**, va faire tes devoirs.
8. Le prof parle trop **vite**. Je **ne** comprends **pratiquement** pas un mot de ce qu'il dit.

4 Complétez le texte avec les mots ci-dessous. Certains mots peuvent être utilisés plusieurs fois.

never • always • hardly ever • then • often • at last • occasionally

"Any plans for tonight, Sam?"
"Well, we don't go to the movies very ... Kate, so why don't we go to a movie for a change? And ..., we could go to a nice restaurant."
"Sounds good! You're right, we ... go to the movies. We ... go to the theatre because you love theatre and you ... ask me what I'd rather do. You're so selfish."
"Don't be silly, Kate! We do go to the movies, well, only ... I must say. And I'm not selfish. You ... say what you want to do, you're ... so busy! How can I possibly guess you'd rather go to the movies?"
"I know, Sam, I know. I should spend less time at the office."
"Wow! You admit it ... ! Better late than never."

5 Complétez avec *again, still, yet* ou *already*.

1. "Is Jessica ... in hospital?"
"Oh, yes. She'll be in hospital for another week."
2. Why did you kick the cat? Don't you ever do that ..., or I'll break your neck.
3. "Where's Mum?"
"She's ... in bed. She came home late last night."
4. "Have you cooked dinner, Adrian?"
"No, not ..., Mum. But Penny's ... set the table, look."
"But, Adrian, you haven't done a thing ... , have you?"
"But Mum! I haven't finished my exams ... ! I'm ... busy, I'm not on holiday! Penny's ... finished her exams."
"Don't tell me ... that you are busy, Adrian. I don't believe it."

SE TESTER

1 1. **b.** They **often had dinner** in that small restaurant downtown.
2. **b.** Ken isn't **brave enough** to leave Barbie. Besides, he doesn't have **enough money** to live on his own.
3. **b.** "**How often** do you go to the gym?" "Twice a week."
4. **c.** Mrs. Parks is a wonderful patient: she **hardly ever** complains.
5. **b.** Two o'clock in the afternoon and he's **still** in bed!
6. **a.** "Has he taken his flight **yet**?" "No, he's **still** waiting at the airport."

S'ENTRAÎNER

2 1. sadly 2. fully 3. desperately 4. unfortunately 5. admirably **(sans e)** 6. fashionably **(sans e)** 7. finally 8. drastic**ally** 9. luck**i**ly 10. seemingly

3 1. "What did he **actually** say?" / "What did he say **actually**?"
"He said that the flat wasn't comfortable **enough**."
2. After seeing the doctor, he **eventually / finally** decided to go on a diet.
3. I'm exhausted. I **badly** need a holiday.
4. Have you seen / Did you see a good play **lately / recently**?
5. Lisa works **well**. She works even **better** than her boss (does).
6. I went to bed **late** last night. I'm working **hard** because I'm taking my exams next week.
7. Let Sophie sleep, and **meanwhile / in the meantime** do your homework.
8. The teacher speaks too **fast**. I **hardly** understand a word he says.

4 "Any plans for tonight, Sam?"
"Well, we don't go to the movies very **often** Kate, so why don't we go to a movie for a change? And **then**, we could go to a nice restaurant."
"Sounds good! You're right, we **hardly ever** go to the movies. We **often / always** go to the theatre because you love theatre and you **never / hardly ever** ask me what I'd rather do. You're so selfish."
"Don't be silly, Kate! We do go to the movies, well, only **occasionally** I must say. And I'm not selfish. You **never** say what you want to do, you're **always** so busy! How can I possibly guess you'd rather go to the movies?"
"I know, Sam, I know. I should spend less time at the office."
"Wow! You admit it **at last**! Better late than never."

5 1. "Is Jessica **still** in hospital?"
"Oh, yes. She'll be in hospital for another week."
2. Why did you kick the cat? Don't you ever do that **again**, or I'll break your neck.
3. "Where's Mum?"
"She's **still** in bed. She came home late last night."
4. "Have you cooked dinner, Adrian?"
"No, not **yet**, Mum. But Penny's **already** set the table, look."
"But, Adrian, you haven't done a thing **yet**, have you?"
"But Mum! I haven't finished my exams **yet**! I'm **still** busy, I'm not on holiday! Penny's **already** finished her exams."
"Don't tell me **again** that you are busy, Adrian. I don't believe it."

CHAPITRE

17 Date, durée, commencement

Pour dire la date, la durée *(for)* ou le commencement *(since)* d'une action ou d'un état, il faut bien choisir le temps des verbes afin que l'on comprenne quand l'événement a eu lieu, a lieu, ou aura lieu. Il faut également maîtriser un certain nombre de mots grammaticaux comme *on, in, at, as, while, ago, for, since*, etc.

I Écrire et dire la date

A Plusieurs possibilités

On écrit...	On dit...
Saturday, January 4th 2013	Saturday, January fourth 2013
Saturday, January 4, 2013	Saturday, January four 2013
Saturday 4 January 2013	Saturday, four January 2013
Saturday, **the** 4th **of** January 2013	Saturday, the fourth of January 2013

ATTENTION !

- N'oubliez pas la majuscule aux noms de jours et de mois.
- Aux États-Unis, le mois précède le jour.

Les attentats du 11 septembre se disent *the terrorist attacks of 9-11 (of nine-eleven).*

Date of birth: 4.12.1996 (12 avril 1996).

B Les ordinaux irréguliers

On écrit...	On dit...
le 1er : (the) 1st	(the) first
le 21e : (the) 21st	(the) twenty-first
le 31e : (the) 31st	(the) thirty-first
le 2e : (the) 2nd	(the) second
le 22e : (the) 22nd	(the) twenty-second
le 3e : (the) 3rd	(the) third
le 23e : (the) 23rd	(the) twenty-third
le 5e : (the) 5th	(the) fifth
le 25e : (the) 25th	(the) twenty-fifth
le 12e : (the) 12th	(the) twelfth

ATTENTION

- *9 (nine) → the ninth* (9e)
- *20 (twenty), 30 (thirty) → the twentieth, the thirtieth* (20e, 30e)

C Dire l'année

1812 : (18 / 12) = eighteen-twelve

1905 : (19 / 05) = nineteen-o-five

2000 : two thousand

2012 : (two thousand / twelve) = two thousand twelve / (20/12) = twenty-twelve

BC /biː'siː/ = Before Christ (avant J.-C.)

46 BC : forty-six BC

AD /eɪ'diː/ = Anno Domini (de notre ère)

57 AD : fifty-seven AD

II Prépositions et conjonctions de temps

- ***As*** **:** quand / comme / tandis que / alors que / au moment (même) où

  She saw the accident **as** she was going to work.
  Elle a vu l'accident en allant / alors qu'elle se rendait au travail.

  As a child, he often played cards.
  Quand il était enfant / Enfant, il jouait souvent aux cartes.

- ***As soon as*** **:** dès que

He called **as soon as** he arrived. Il a téléphoné dès qu'il est arrivé.

I'll shower **as soon as** I **get** home. (contrairement au français : verbe au **présent**)
Je me doucherai dès que j'arriverai à la maison.

I'll call you **as soon as** I **have spoken** to the doctor. *(present perfect)*
Je t'appellerai dès que j'aurai parlé au médecin.

- ***At***

at five o'clock

at Christmas / Easter (à Noël / Pâques)

at night (la nuit)

late **at** night

at the beginning / **at** the end of…

- ***Before / after***

I met Lola **before / after** the party. J'ai rencontré Lola avant / après la soirée.

I spoke to Liz **before / after** I spoke to Tom.
J'ai parlé à Liz avant d'avoir / après avoir parlé à Tom.

Before / After speak**ing** to the Prime Minister, Wilson called his wife.
Avant de parler / Après avoir parlé au Premier ministre, Wilson a téléphoné à sa femme.

Please phone me **before / after** Jody **comes** back.
Appelle-moi avant / après le retour de Jody.

- ***By*** **:** avant / d'ici

I want you to be home **by** ten.
Je veux que tu sois rentré pour dix heures / à dix heures dernier délai.

By the end of the day, Jasper felt much better.
En fin de journée, Jasper se sentait beaucoup mieux.

By the time I got there, Paul had gone.
Le temps que j'arrive, Paul était parti.

It will be too late **by** the time you **get** there. (contrairement au français : verbe au **présent**)
Le temps que tu arrives, il sera trop tard.

- ***During*** **+ nom ou groupe nominal :** pendant + nom ou groupe nominal

They met **during** the holidays. Ils se sont rencontrés pendant les vacances.

ATTENTION !
Pendant trois heures, deux jours, six ans, etc. : **for** three hours, **for** two days, **for** six years, etc. car il s'agit d'une durée.

- ***In***

moment de la journée : **in** the morning, **early in** the morning, **in** late afternoon, **in** the (middle of) the night

mois : **in** February

saison : **in** (the) spring

année : **in** 1938

décennie (decade) : **in** the 1980s

siècle (century) : **in** the 18th century

- ***On*** **+ jour**

I'll see you **on** the 10th.

She's coming **on** Friday.

He was born **on** April 6th 2007.

We'll see you **on** Christmas Eve (le 24 décembre).

- ***Until / till*** : jusqu'à (ce que)

Till est moins formel que *until.*

They stayed **until / till** midnight. Ils sont restés jusqu'à minuit.

She cried **until / till** Roddy came back. Elle a pleuré jusqu'au retour de Roddy.

*I'll work **until / till** the film **is** ready.* (contrairement au français : verbe au **présent**)
Je travaillerai jusqu'à ce que le film soit prêt.

ATTENTION !
« Avant » ne se traduit pas toujours par *before*.
I won't be free **until** the 10th. Je **ne** serai **pas** libre **avant** le 10.

- ***While*** **+ groupe verbal** : pendant que

They split up **while** they **were** holiday**ing** in Italy.
Ils ont rompu pendant qu'ils étaient en vacances en Italie.

EXPRESSIONS À RETENIR

demain : tomorrow
le lendemain : the next day, the following day, the day after
après-demain : the day after tomorrow, in two days from now
hier : yesterday
la veille : the day before
la semaine prochaine : Ø next week
la semaine suivante : the next / the following week / the week after
le mois dernier : Ø last month
le dernier mois : the last month

III Traduire « il y a… » (passé) : *ago* + prétérit

Jack et Alice **se sont rencontrés** il y a cinq ans. Jack and Alice **met** five years **ago**.

Ici, c'est le moment de la rencontre qui compte. Cette rencontre appartient au **passé**, même si Jack et Alice se voient toujours : verbe au **prétérit**.

IV Exprimer la durée et le temps écoulé : *for*

A Durée

For fonctionne avec tous les temps.

I **worked for** fifteen hours **yesterday**! J'ai travaillé (pendant) quinze heures hier !

She **sleeps for** a couple of hours **every afternoon**. Elle dort deux ou trois heures chaque après-midi.

He**'ll** stay here **for** three weeks. Il va passer trois semaines ici.

B Temps écoulé

- En français, pour évoquer le temps qui s'est écoulé, on peut dire :

  Il y a cinq ans **que** Jack et Alice se connaissent.

  Cela / Ça fait cinq ans **que** Jack et Alice se connaissent.

  Jack et Alice **se connaissent depuis** cinq ans.

- En anglais, on dit alors :

  Jack and Alice **have known** each other for five years. toujours vrai → *present perfect*

V Indiquer le point de départ d'une action ou d'un état : *since*

Dans les phrases suivantes, ce n'est pas la durée qui compte, mais **le point de départ** (début, commencement) de l'action ou de l'état → ***since.***

Ben **habite** à Dublin depuis 2004.
Ben **has been living** in Dublin **since** 2004.
Ici, toujours vrai → *present perfect* début

Tim **est** très heureux depuis qu'il travaille pour Mr Bell.
Tim **has been** very happy **since** he **has been working** for Mr Bell.
Ici, toujours vrai → *present perfect* début ici, toujours vrai → *present perfect*

Bill **est** grincheux depuis qu'il **a échoué** à son permis de conduire.
Bill **has been** grumpy **since** he fail**ed** his driving test.
Ici, toujours vrai → *present perfect* début événement passé → prétérit

ATTENTION !

- Pour traduire « **depuis** », vous devez donc vous demander s'il s'agit du « depuis » qui exprime une **durée** → ***for*** ou du « depuis » qui indique le point de départ, le **commencement** d'une action ou d'un état → ***since***.
Dans ce type de phrases, le *present perfect* se traduit souvent par un présent, et le *past perfect* par un imparfait.
- Au passé, le prétérit et le *present perfect* se transforment en ***past perfect***.
Ben **had been living** in Dublin since 2004 (when he met Emily).
Tim **had been** very happy since he **had been working** for Mr Bell (and he was shocked when he was fired).
Bill **had been** grumpy since he **had** fail**ed** his driving test.

RÉCAPITULONS

- **Ordinaux** : notez bien l'orthographe de fifth, eighth, ninth, twelfth... ainsi que la transformation du y en i : twenty → twentieth / thirty → thirtieth...
- Since marque le point de départ d'une action ou d'un état.
- For marque la durée et le temps écoulé .
- Ago n'accompagne que des événements entièrement révolus.

SE TESTER QUIZ

1 Choisissez la bonne solution.

1. It's my grandparents' ... wedding anniversary today.
☐ **a.** fortieth ☐ **b.** fortyeth ☐ **c.** fourtieth

2. She wrote this song two months ... .
☐ **a.** before ☐ **b.** ago ☐ **c.** since

3. He fell asleep ... the concert.
☐ **a.** for ☐ **b.** since ☐ **c.** during

4. I haven't heard from him ... ages.
☐ **a.** since ☐ **b.** for ☐ **c.** before

5. It's been quite cold ... the beginning of the month.
☐ **a.** since ☐ **b.** for ☐ **c.** as soon as

6. She was quiet ... ten seconds and then she started screaming again.
☐ **a.** during ☐ **b.** for ☐ **c.** since

S'ENTRAÎNER

2 Écrivez les dates ci-dessous en toutes lettres.

1492 1776 1863 1917 1963 2001

3 Traduisez.

1. Le 6 février, il se réveilla à 11 heures. Le lendemain, il se réveilla à midi.
2. Si nous ne pouvons pas aller au cinéma la semaine prochaine, nous irons la semaine suivante.
3. Je suis allé aux Pays-Bas le mois dernier.
4. La dernière semaine fut un désastre. Je voulais rentrer à la maison le plus vite possible.

4 Complétez. Là où il n'y a rien à ajouter, inscrivez Ø.

1. Rebecca was born ... October 22nd ... 2006.
2. Give mummy a kiss ... you go to bed.
3. I always go to bed late ... night.
4. They got there ... the afternoon.
5. He moved to Chicago ... the 1990s.
6. OK, you may go. But you'd better be back ... midnight.

7. Don't worry, I'll have tidied the flat ... the time you come back.
8. I'll stay ... Daisy comes back. I'd love to see her.
9. Daisy won't be back ... 7 p.m.
10. Tom was lying in the sun ... his mother was ironing his shirts.

5 Traduisez.

1. Clara watched TV for ten hours yesterday.
2. I have known him for six years.
3. Phil has been depressed since his wife left him.
4. Jack had been much more serene since he had found a new job.

SE TESTER

1 1. **a.** It's my grandparents' **fortieth** wedding anniversary today.
2. **b.** She wrote this song two months **ago**.
3. **c.** He fell asleep **during** the concert.
4. **b.** I haven't heard from him **for** ages.
5. **a.** It's been quite cold **since** the beginning of the month.
6. **b.** She was quiet **for** ten seconds, and then she started screaming again.

S'ENTRAÎNER

2 **1492:** fourteen-ninety-two (Discovery of America by Christopher Columbus)
1776: seventeen-seventy-six (on July 4, the American Declaration of Independence from Britain)
1863: eighteen-sixty-three (Emancipation Act, thanks to President Lincoln)
1917: nineteen-seventeen (the USA joined the allied forces in World War I)
1963: nineteen-sixty-three (Martin Luther King Jr. organised a huge march on Washington D.C. to promote racial harmony; President Kennedy was assassinated in Dallas)
2001: two-thousand-one (the 9/11 terrorist attacks in the USA)

3 1. **On February 6th / On the 6th of February,** he woke up **at 11 (a.m.).** The following day he woke up **at 12 / at noon.**
2. If we can't go to the cinema / to the movies **next week**, we'll go **the following week / the week after**.
3. I went to the Netherlands **last month**.
4. **The last week** was horrible / was a disaster. I wanted to go home **as soon as** possible.

4 1. Rebecca was born **on** October 22nd **Ø** 2006.
2. Give mummy a kiss **before** you go to bed.
3. I always go to bed late **at** night.
4. They got there **in** the afternoon.
5. He moved to Chicago **in** the 1990s.
6. OK, you may go. But you'd better be back **by** midnight.
7. Don't worry, I'll have tidied the flat **by** the time you come back.
8. I'll stay **until / till** Daisy comes back. I'd love to see her.
9. Daisy won't be back **until / till** 7 p.m.
10. Tom was lying in the sun **while** his mother was ironing his shirts.

5 1. Clara a regardé la télé pendant dix heures hier.
2. Ça / Cela fait six ans que je le connais. / Je le connais depuis six ans.
3. Phil est déprimé depuis que sa femme l'a quitté.
4. Jack était beaucoup plus serein depuis qu'il avait retrouvé du travail.

CHAPITRE

18 Présent et passé

Il n'existe que deux temps en anglais : le présent et le passé.

I Présent simple et prétérit simple

A Présent simple

- Habitude

  I **get** up at six every morning.

- Actions successives, décrites « en direct »

  He **rushes** to the door, **kicks** it open and **shouts**: "Out!"
  Il se rue vers la porte, l'ouvre d'un coup de pied et hurle : « Dehors ! »

- Vérité générale, fait établi

  The sun **rises** in the East.

- Caractéristique du sujet

  She **likes** sweets and chocolates.

- Fait à venir (→ p. 193)

  My train **leaves** at fives.

B Prétérit simple

- Renvoi au passé (temps du récit par excellence)

  Shakespeare **wrote** his first tragedies in the 1590s.
  Shakespeare écrivit ses premières tragédies dans les années 1590.

  He **died** thirty years ago.
  Il est mort il y a trente ans.

ATTENTION !
Après un verbe introducteur (say, tell, annouce…) au prétérit, on emploie généralement le prétérit pour rapporter des paroles prononcées à ce moment-là.
He said he **wanted** to talk to me. Il m'a dit qu'il voulait me parler.

- Renvoi à l'irréel, à l'hypothétique. Ce type de prétérit est dit « modal ».

If you **worked** harder, you would succeed.
Si tu travaillais davantage, tu réussirais.

I wish he **listened** to me!
Si seulement il m'écoutait !

I'd rather she **didn't** speak that way.
Je préférerais qu'elle ne parle pas de cette façon.

II Présent en *-ing* et prétérit en *-ing*

A Présent en *-ing*

- Action en cours (= inachevée) au moment où l'on parle

I can't talk to you: I'**m marking** those papers.
Je ne peux pas te parler : je corrige ces copies.

- Description

In the painting *The Card Players* by Cézanne, there are four men. One **is standing** while the other three **are sitting** around a table and **are playing** cards.
Dans le tableau de Cézanne intitulé *Les Joueurs de cartes*, il y a quatre hommes : un se tient debout tandis que les trois autres sont assis autour d'une table et jouent aux cartes.

- Renvoi à l'avenir (intention, planification → p. 193)

Tom and Lola **are getting** married next year.
Tom et Lola se marient / vont se marier l'année prochaine.

- Expression d'un point de vue du locuteur : agacement, désapprobation ou approbation (selon le contexte)

Look at her! She **is smoking** again!
Non mais, regarde-la ! Elle continue à fumer. (Quelle honte !)

She's a lovely baby. She'**s** always smil**ing**!
C'est un bébé adorable. Elle n'arrête pas de sourire. (Comme c'est agréable !)

B Prétérit en *-ing*

- Action en cours dans le passé

  Audrey **was reading** while Frank **was watching** television.
  Audrey lisait tandis que Frank regardait la télévision.

- Description dans le passé

  She **was shaking** with anger.
  Elle tremblait de colère.

- Renvoi à l'avenir : événement « planifié » dans une narration au passé

  When he **arrived**, he learnt that Tom and Lola **were getting** married in July.
  Lorsqu'il arriva, il apprit que Tom et Lola **allaient se marier** en juillet.

- Expression d'un point de vue du locuteur sur un événement passé : agacement, désapprobation ou approbation (selon le contexte)

  My brother was a pain in the neck. He **was** always **complaining**! (*Always* sera fortement accentué à l'oral.)
  Mon frère était une vraie plaie. Il **fallait toujours** qu'il se plaigne !

C Présent simple ou présent en *-ing* ?

Certains verbes se rencontrent plus rarement à la forme *-ing*. Il s'agit des « verbes d'état » *(be, exist, deserve, cost, expect, have...)*, des verbes qui renvoient à un processus mental *(know, think, imagine, agree, believe, remember, suppose...)* et des verbes de perception involontaire *(hear, smell, see...)*. Quand ils prennent la forme en *-ing*, ces verbes changent souvent de sens.

He **is** stupid.
Il **est** idiot.

He **is being** stupid.
Il **fait** l'idiot.

She **sees** him in the distance.
Elle le **voit** au loin.

She **is seeing** him tonight.
Elle **a rendez-vous** avec lui ce soir.

D Prétérit simple ou prétérit en *-ing* ?

Le prétérit simple renvoie à des faits « bruts », ponctuels, précis.
Le prétérit en *-ing* montre l'événement passé dans son déroulement.

Tom **was ironing** his shirts when Lola **proposed** to him.
Tom repassait ses chemises quand Lola le demanda en mariage.

III *Present perfect* simple et *past perfect* simple

A *Present perfect* simple : bilan, résultat

Pour souligner les **conséquences**, les **résultats actuels d'un événement** passé ou toujours en cours de réalisation (inachevé), on utilise le ***present perfect* simple**.

Your nose is bleeding. **Has** somebody **hit** you?
Tu saignes du nez. Quelqu'un t'a frappé ?

I'**ve worked** here for a long time.
Je travaille ici depuis longtemps. / Cela fait longtemps que je travaille ici.

B *Past perfect* simple

- Valeur de **passé antérieur**

When Alex saw Peter, he realized they **had met** before.
Quand Alex vit Peter, il se rendit compte qu'ils s'**étaient déjà rencontrés**.

- Valeur de **bilan** ou de **résultat dans le passé**

She wore a bandage because she **had sprained** her ankle.
Elle portrait un bandage parce qu'elle s'était foulé la cheville.

I **had known** him for 10 years when he became famous.
Cela faisait dix ans que je le connaissais quand il devint célèbre.

> Après un verbe introducteur au prétérit, on emploie le *past perfect* pour rapporter des paroles prononcées dans un passé antérieur.
> "I stole the car," she admitted. → She admitted she **had stolen** the car.

- Renvoi à l'**irréel du passé**, à l'**hypothétique** (valeur de regret ou de reproche, selon le contexte)

I wish you **had told** me.
Je regrette que tu ne me l'aies pas dit.

If only I **had known**!
Si seulement j'avais su!

I'd rather you **hadn't come**!
J'aurais préféré que tu ne viennes pas !

C Prétérit simple ou *present perfect* simple ?

■ Le prétérit simple et en *-ing* montre qu'une action ou un état sont révolus. L'une des fonctions du *present perfect* simple est de souligner un lien étroit entre un **fait passé** et son **résultat** ou ses **conséquences** dans le présent.

I've finished this book: you can have it now.
J'ai terminé ce livre : tu peux le prendre.

■ Comme le *present perfect* simple est intimement lié au moment présent, on le rencontre souvent avec les adverbes ou les expressions qui établissent un lien entre le passé et le présent : *already, yet, ever, never, lately, recently, it's the first time*. On le rencontre aussi avec *how long, for* et *since* quand on fait le bilan d'une durée.

"Have you **ever** heard of Rosa Parks?"
"**No, it's the first time** I've heard of her."
« As-tu jamais entendu parler de Rosa Parks ? »
« Non, c'est la première fois que j'entends parler d'elle. »

Notez **ici** la traduction du *present perfect* par un présent en français.

IV *Present perfect* en *-ing* et *past perfect* en *-ing*

A *Present perfect* en *-ing*

■ Action commencée dans le passé, en cours de réalisation, inachevée au moment où l'on parle

James? He's been sleeping all day!
James ? Il a passé sa journée à dormir. (et il dort encore)

■ Action (à peine) terminée mais **dont les résultats sont bien visibles** dans le présent (valeur d'insistance)

Have you been gardening all day? You look exhausted.
As-tu passé la journée à jardiner ? Tu as l'air épuisé.

■ Mise en valeur de la durée écoulée (souvent associée à *for* ou *since*)

She**'s been working** on that book for years!
Cela fait des années qu'elle travaille à ce livre !

He **has been living** in San Francisco since the 1960s.
Il vit à San Francisco depuis les années 60.

Notez **ici** la traduction du *present perfect* en *-ing* par un présent en français.

Avec never, always, all my life ou un nombre précis, le present perfect simple est obligatoire.

I've never **driven**.

He's **worked** there all his life.

She **has** always **lived** in Oxford.

We'**ve written** five letters.

- Expression d'insistance (qui, selon le contexte, peut exprimer la joie, l'agacement, l'approbation ou la désapprobation)

  Have you been cleaning the windows? You're a darling!
  Tu as nettoyé les vitres ? Tu es un amour !

B *Past perfect* en *-ing*

On retrouve avec le *past perfect* en *-ing* **les mêmes valeurs** que celles du *present perfect* en *-ing*, **mais dans le passé**.

We'**d been driving** for about an hour when a storm broke out.
Nous roulions depuis environ une heure quand un orage éclata.

When I met him, he **had been living** in San Francisco since the 1960s.
Quand je l'ai rencontré, il vivait à San Francisco depuis les années 60.

Comme pour le present perfect simple, avec never, always, all my life ou un chiffre précis, la forme simple est obligatoire.

She **had** always **lived** in that small village.

C *Present perfect* simple ou *present perfect* en *-ing* ?

Le *present perfect* simple exprime plutôt un **bilan**, un **résultat** actuel, alors que le *present perfect* en *-ing* insiste sur la **période écoulée**.

Prices **have increased** by 10%.
Prices **have been increasing** by 10%.

Dans le premier cas, seul le résultat compte (maintenant les prix sont plus élevés). Dans le deuxième cas, c'est le processus qui est souligné et le fait qu'il n'est pas terminé (les prix continuent à augmenter).

La forme -ing est rare avec certains verbes (verbes d'état, de perception involontaire ou renvoyant à un processus mental). Ainsi, même si l'action se poursuit au moment où je parle, on dira :
He'**s loved** football ever since he met Beckham.
Il aime le football depuis le jour où il a rencontré Beckham.

D *Past perfect* simple ou *past perfect* en *-ing* ?

Le *past perfect* simple indique l'**antériorité** de l'événement par rapport à un autre événement lui-même passé. Le *past perfect* simple peut également souligner dans un contexte passé le **résultat** d'un événement sur un autre.
Le *past perfect* en *-ing* s'intéresse davantage au **déroulement de l'action**.

I'**d been watching** the news when the TV exploded.
Je **regardais** les informations quand la télévision a explosé.

La remarque sur la forme en -ing peu compatible avec certains verbes est valable ici aussi :
How long **had** you **known** him when he married Julia?
Cela faisait combien de temps que tu le connaissais quand il a épousé Julia ?

RÉCAPITULONS

- Avant de choisir une forme verbale, examinez la situation : s'agit-il de quelque chose d'habituel, de général ? En cours de réalisation, temporaire ? Ne calquez pas sur le français.
- Dans *present perfect*, il y a le mot *present*. Le *present perfect* est tout sauf un temps du passé, soit parce qu'il permet de faire un bilan (*I've never met him*), soit parce que le moment présent est inclus (*I've been waiting for two hours!*).

SE TESTER QUIZ

1 Choisissez la bonne solution.

1. I ... when you phoned.
- ☐ **a.** slept ☐ **b.** was sleeping ☐ **c.** have been sleeping

2. It is a well-known fact that most children ... fast.
- ☐ **a.** learn ☐ **b.** are learning ☐ **c.** had been learning

3. How often ... tennis?
- ☐ **a.** have you been playing ☐ **b.** were you playing ☐ **c.** do you play

4. I ... too fast, I am out of breath now.
- ☐ **a.** 've been running ☐ **b.** had run ☐ **c.** had been running

5. The kids ... for hours. They must be tired!
- ☐ **a.** are playing ☐ **b.** have been playing ☐ **c.** played

6. I could tell she ... the moment I saw her.
- ☐ **a.** cried ☐ **b.** had been crying ☐ **c.** has been crying

S'ENTRAÎNER

2 Mettez les verbes en gras au présent simple ou au présent en *-ing* et justifiez votre réponse.

1. **a.** I **(see)** you're cheating *(tricher)* again.
b. He **(see)** Andrew tomorrow.

2. **a.** John **(be)** a great tennis player.
b. Stop it, Jess! You **(be)** silly now.

3. **a.** Don't disturb me: I **(read)** Mary Higgins Clark's latest novel.
b. Sam **(read)** at least two books a week.

4. **a.** I **(think)** she lives in Paris.
b. She **(think)** about her exams again. Look at her face!

5. **a.** "I had a bad day at the office today".
"Oh, come on! You **(complain / always)** about your job!"
b. Tourists usually **(complain)** about prices in London.

6. **a.** He **(have)** three digital cameras.
b. Don't disturb her. She **(have)** a shower.

3 **Mettez les verbes en gras au prétérit simple ou au *present perfect* simple. Justifiez votre choix.**

1. "Wow! You **(put on)** weight!"
"Well, I **(eat)** a lot of junk food when I was in America."
2. Since I **(stop)** smoking, my health **(improve)**.
3. I recognized him the moment I **(see)** him.
4. As soon as he **(hear)** footsteps in the stairs, the dog barked *(aboyer)*.
5. I **(finish)** my homework at last: I can have a rest now!

4 **Mettez les verbes en gras au prétérit simple ou au *past perfect* simple. Justifiez vos choix.**

1. Nothing would have happened if you **(be)** a little more cautious.
2. When I saw this house for the first time, I knew I **(find)** exactly what I wanted.
3. She **(push)** the door open and **(walk)** into the room.
4. If only you **(tell)** me! I would have been able to help you.
5. The alarm **(go)** off when he **(try)** to push that door.
6. Harry was late that morning because he **(forget)** his keys.

5 **Mettez les verbes entre parenthèses aux temps et à la forme qui conviennent.**

POUR VOUS AIDER
Lisez bien le texte dans son intégralité en repérant tous les indices susceptibles de vous aider avant de commencer l'exercice.

"I remember when I first (discover) the idea of *moments*. It (be) my birthday, I must have been fourteen or fifteen and my folks (take) me to Staten Island to spend the day at the fairgrounds. It (be) a Saturday, but for some reason my dad (have to) leave at noon to check something out at his factory in the Bronx. I remember standing on the pier and waving good-bye to him as the ferry (pull out). I (look) around at the crowd, everybody (wave) to some person on the boat, and I suddenly (realize) this was a *moment*. [...] The ferry (pull out), (maneuvre), (turn) in the harbor, (gather) speed. We kept on waving. My dad (wear) a red sweater that day, so he (stand) out in the crowd on deck. We could see his little red arm moving up and down, getting smaller and smaller as the ferry (recede) into the distance...

folks: parents
pier: appontement
pull out: faire machine arrière
gather speed: prendre de la vitesse
recede: s'éloigner

Nancy Huston, *Dolce Agonia*, 2002.

SE TESTER

1 1. **b.** I was sleeping when you phoned.
2. **a.** It is a well-known fact that most children learn fast.
3. **c.** How often do you play tennis?
4. **a.** I've been running too fast, I am out of breath now.
5. **b.** The kids have been playing for hours. They must be tired!
6. **b.** I could tell she had been crying the moment I saw her.

S'ENTRAÎNER

2 1. **a.** see (perception) **b.** is seeing (avoir rendez-vous ; futur)
2. **a.** is (caractéristique du sujet) **b.** are being (comportement temporaire + reproche)
3. **a.** am reading (action en cours) **b.** reads (habitude)
4. **a.** think (opinion) **b.** is thinking (réfléchir)
5. **a.** are always complaining (tu n'arrêtes pas de te plaindre ; reproche, irritation) **b.** complain (caractéristique / habitude)
6. **a.** has (posséder) **b.** is having (prendre une douche ; action en cours)

3 1. you've put on (bilan) / I ate (action révolue)
2. stopped / has improved (action révolue / résultat) 3. saw (action révolue)
4. heard (action révolue) 5. I've finished (bilan)

4 1. had been (antériorité, concordance des temps)
2. had found (bilan, résultat dans le passé)
3. pushed / walked (actions ponctuelles et successives dans le passé)
4. had told (*if only* + *past perfect* = reproche)
5. went / tried (actions ponctuelles et révolues)
6. had forgotten (antériorité)

5 I remember when I first discovered the idea of *moments*. It was my birthday, I must have been fourteen or fifteen and my folks had taken me to Staten Island to spend the day at the fairgrounds. It was a Saturday, but for some reason my dad had to leave at noon [...]. I remember standing on the pier and waving good-bye to him as the ferry pulled out. I looked around at the crowd, everybody was waving to some person on the boat, and I suddenly realized this was a *moment*. [...] The ferry pulled out, maneuvered, turned in the harbor, gathered speed. We kept on waving. My dad was wearing a red sweater that day, so he stood out in the crowd on deck. We could see his little red arm moving up and down [...] as the ferry receded into the distance...

CHAPITRE

19 La référence à l'avenir

Pour renvoyer à l'avenir, on a recours aux auxiliaires de modalité *will* et *shall*, au présent simple ou en *-ing* et à d'autres structures : *be going to*, *be about to*, etc.

I *Will* et *shall*

A Généralités

■ ***Will*** et ***shall*** permettent de renvoyer à l'avenir, mais, étant des auxiliaires de modalité, ils peuvent aussi exprimer d'autres nuances : volonté, promesse, refus, etc. (→ p. 208).

Don't worry, he'**ll** come back.
Ne t'inquiète pas, il reviendra.

I **shall** be here in a minute.
J'arrive tout de suite. (c'est promis)

Will est souvent contracté *('ll / won't)*.

■ ***Shall***, beaucoup plus rare, se rencontre essentiellement avec ***I*** et ***we***. Notez sa forme négative : *shan't*.

B Principales valeurs

■ **Simple référence à l'avenir : *will* + base verbale**

She'**ll** succeed, I'm sure!

"**Will** you be there?" "No I **won't**. Sorry."

■ **Décision prise par le locuteur**

"Heck! I've lost my wallet."
"Don't worry, I'**ll** lend you some money."
« Zut ! J'ai perdu mon portefeuille. » « Ne t'inquiète pas, je **vais** te prêter de l'argent. »

■ **Projection : *will / shall* + *be* + V *-ing***

This time next week, I'**ll be flying** to Miami.
À la même heure la semaine prochaine, je serai dans l'avion pour Miami.

II Présent simple et en *-ing*

On emploie le présent simple ou en *-ing* pour évoquer un programme, un horaire, un événement planifié (→ p. 182-183).
La forme en *-ing* est plus courante avec un sujet animé.

This course **starts** next week. Ce stage démarre la semaine prochaine.

Justin **is getting** married next year. Justin se marie l'année prochaine.

III Autres formulations

- **Intention du locuteur, événement prévisible : *be going to* + V**

I'**m going to** stop smoking.
Je vais arrêter de fumer.

Look at those clouds! It'**s going** to rain again!
Regarde un peu ces nuages, il va encore pleuvoir!

> *Be going to* n'évoque pas forcément un futur proche. Il est beaucoup plus rare que « aller faire quelque chose » en français.

- **Imminence : *be about to* + V**

Hurry up! We'**re about to** start!
Dépêche-toi ! On est sur le point de commencer !

- **Engagement : *be to* + V**

Sophie **is to pick up** the boss at the airport this afternoon.
Sophie doit aller chercher / Il est prévu que Sophie aille chercher le patron à l'aéroport cet après-midi.

IV Renvoi au futur dans un contexte au passé

- ***Will* → *would***

I **was** sure they **would** come. J'étais sûr qu'ils viendraient.

- ***Be going to* → *was / were going to***

I **knew** she **was going to** leave me. Je savais qu'elle allait me quitter.

- ***Be about to* → *was / were about to***

I **was about to** leave when I **got** a call. J'étais sur le point de partir quand j'ai reçu un appel.

- ***Be to* → *was / were to***

She **was to** call me back two hours later. Elle devait me rappeler deux heures plus tard.

She **was to** meet her husband in Italy. Elle devait rencontrer son mari en Italie.

V Les subordonnées de temps

■ Quand *when, as soon as, as long as, until, once, after, before, whenever* introduisent une **subordonnée de temps**, *will* n'apparaît jamais.

• **Présent simple**

Phone me **when** you **0 get** there. Téléphone-moi quand tu **seras** arrivé.

I'll have a word with Alice before she goes to Sam's party.
Je dirai deux mots à Alice avant qu'elle aille à la soirée de Sam.

• ***Present perfect***

Il permet de souligner l'aspect accompli.

I'll help you **once** I **have finished** my homework.
Je t'aiderai quand / une fois que j'**aurai fini** mes devoirs.

■ Dans une question directe *(When will he come home?)*, ou une proposition complément d'objet de la principale *(I don't know when he will come home)*, on utilise ***will***.

RÉCAPITULONS

■ Il n'y a pas de temps « futur » en anglais, mais plusieurs formulations faisant référence à l'avenir, chacune étant associée à une nuance particulière.
■ Pas de futur (will / shall) dans les subordonnées de temps.

SE TESTER QUIZ

1 Choisissez la bonne solution.

1. When you … this letter, I'll be far away.
- [ ] **a.** will read
- [ ] **b.** shall read
- [ ] **c.** read

2. Mrs. Daniels … kill me if I'm late again!
- [ ] **a.** is going to
- [ ] **b.** is to
- [ ] **c.** will

3. All the arrangements have been made. We … tomorrow.
- [ ] **a.** will leave
- [ ] **b.** are leaving
- [ ] **c.** are going to leave

4. Hurry up! The film … .
- [ ] **a.** is to start
- [ ] **b.** will start
- [ ] **c.** is about to start

5. You'd better hurry! Your article … by midnight, remember.
- [ ] **a.** will be completed
- [ ] **b.** is to be completed
- [ ] **c.** is going to be completed

6. Once you … those horrible exams, studying will be a piece of cake.
- [ ] **a.** will take
- [ ] **b.** have taken
- [ ] **c.** shall take

S'ENTRAÎNER

2 Traduisez les phrases suivantes.

1. Quand tu liras cette lettre, il sera trop tard.
2. Tant que tu resteras ici, tu seras en sécurité.
3. Chaque fois que tu auras besoin de moi, tu m'appelleras.
4. Dès que j'aurai terminé ce livre, j'en commencerai un autre.
5. Je me demande quand Bob passera son permis !

3 Dans ces phrases, déterminez la valeur du futur, puis traduisez.

1. Ce train quitte Paddington à 9 heures précises.
2. « Je ne comprends pas cet exercice d'anglais ! »
« Pas de panique, tu sais bien que je vais t'aider ! »
3. À la même date, l'année prochaine, mes parents célèbreront leur 20e anniversaire de mariage *(wedding anniversary)*.
4. J'étais sur le point de l'embrasser quand elle m'a dit qu'elle était mariée.
5. J'ai fait mes bagages *(pack one's luggage)*. Je m'envole pour Moscou demain.
6. Regarde-le : il va encore se mettre en colère *(lose one's temper)*.
7. Ces documents doivent être prêts pour demain : je l'ai promis au patron.
8. Lisez soigneusement ce livre et vous deviendrez un génie !

SE TESTER

1 1. **c.** When you **read** this letter, I'll be far away.
2. **c.** Mrs. Daniels **will** kill me if I'm late again!
3. **b.** All the arrangements have been made. We **are leaving** tomorrow.
4. **c.** Hurry up! The film **is about to start**.
5. **b.** You'd better hurry! Your article **is to be completed** by midnight, remember.
6. **b.** Once you **have taken** those horrible exams, studying will be a piece of cake.

S'ENTRAÎNER

2 1. When you read this letter, it'll be too late.
2. As long as you stay here, you'll be safe.
3. Whenever you need me, give me a call.
4. As soon as I've finished this book, I'll start a new one.
5. I wonder when Bob will take his driving license!

3 1. This train **leaves** from Paddington at 9 o'clock sharp. **Horaire**
2. "I don't understand this English exercise!"
"Don't panic, you know I'**m going to** help you." **Intention**
3. Same date next year, my parents **will be celebrating** their 20th wedding anniversary. **Projection**
4. I **was about to** kiss her when she told me she was married. **Action imminente dans le passé**
5. I've packed my luggage. I'**m flying** / I **fly** to Moscow tomorrow. **Événement planifié**
6. Look at him: he'**s going to** lose his temper again. **Événement prévisible**
7. These documents **are to** be ready by tomorrow. I've promised the manager. **Valeur d'engagement**
8. Read this book carefully and you'**ll** become a genius. **Simple référence à l'avenir**

CHAPITRE

20 Le passif

Il n'y a pas de construction passive sans l'auxiliaire *be*, qui doit être conjugué : *Nell was fired by her boss ; Dan will be helped by John and Tim*. Le passif peut aussi signaler que l'agent (l'auteur de l'action) est inconnu ou a peu d'importance : *Our school has been vandalized ; This table was bought in Italy*.

I Formation

- Le passif se construit avec ***be* + participe passé**. (Il est indispensable de connaître les verbes irréguliers → rabat arrière.) Quand le **complément d'agent** est mentionné, il est introduit par ***by***.

  The snake **was killed by** a neighbour.
  Le serpent a été tué par un voisin.

  I **was asked** to meet them at the station.
  On m'a demandé de les retrouver / accueillir à la gare.

- Le passif est assez fréquent en anglais et il peut être associé à tous les temps et à toutes les formes.

  The instructions **are given** in English.
  Les instructions sont données en anglais.

  They could **be arrested** for arson.
  Ils pourraient être arrêtés pour incendie volontaire.

  All the alumni **had been gathered** on that occasion.
  Tous les anciens élèves avaient été réunis pour cette occasion.

  He likes **being admired**.
  Il aime qu'on l'admire.

  He seemed to **have been shaken**.
  Il semblait avoir été secoué.

  A lot of money **is being spent** to renovate the building.
  On dépense beaucoup d'argent pour rénover ce bâtiment.

II Emplois

- Le passif s'emploie avec presque tous les verbes **transitifs** (verbes suivis d'un complément d'objet).

Actif : They elected him in 2007.

Passif : He was elected in 2007. Il a été élu en 2007.

- **Les verbes prépositionnels et / ou à particule**

Ce sont des verbes dont le complément est introduit par une **préposition** ou qui sont suivis d'une **particule**. Au passif, la préposition et / ou la particule se placent juste **après le participe passé**. Presque tous les verbes prépositionnels ou à particule peuvent être mis au passif.

Jane looks **after** my children. → My children are looked **after** by Jane.
C'est Jane qui s'occupe de mes enfants.

Someone broke **into** my office. → My office was broken **into**.
On est entré par effraction dans mon bureau.

Her grandfather brought her **up**. → She was brought **up** by her grandfather.
Elle a été élevée par son grand-père.

- **Structures particulières**

• **Verbes à double complément** : il s'agit de verbes suivis de deux compléments, le premier (1) étant complément d'attribution, le second (2) complément d'objet direct.

My dad bought me (1) a new bike (2).

→ I was bought a new bike (by my dad).

→ A new bike was bought **for** me (by my dad).

Dans la première structure passive, c'est la personne qui est mise en avant ; dans la seconde, il s'agit du cadeau. Si, en théorie, les deux structures sont possibles, la seconde reste cependant exceptionnelle.

• **Verbes exprimant une opinion, une croyance, une information** *(believe, consider, declare, expect, know, say, suppose, think, etc.)*

People think smoking is bad for your health. → Smoking **is thought to be** bad for your health.
On pense que fumer est mauvais pour la santé.

ATTENTION !

Veillez à la concordance des temps.

People believed that the terrorists **had fled** abroad.

→ The terrorists were believed **to have fled** abroad.

On pensait que les terroristes s'étaient enfuis à l'étranger.

- **Verbes suivis d'une forme en *-ing***

  The teacher caught them cheating. → They **were caught** cheating by the teacher.
  Ils ont été pris en train de tricher par le professeur.

- ***Make* + V**

  They made him work hard. → He **was made to** work hard.

- **Traduction de verbes pronominaux**

  It **isn't done**. Ça ne **se** fait pas.

  It **is** wash**ed** cold. Ça **se** lave à l'eau froide.

III Valeurs

Dans les constructions passives, l'objet de l'action se trouve en tête de phrase ou de proposition, ce qui le **met en valeur**. Comparez :

The decision has deprived many people of the right to vote.
Cette décision a privé beaucoup de gens de leur droit de vote. (insistance sur la décision)

Many people have **be**en depriv**ed** of the right to vote by the decision.
Beaucoup de gens ont été privés de leur droit de vote à cause de cette décision. (insistance sur les personnes)

Complément d'agent ou pas ?

- On s'abstiendra de mentionner un complément d'agent quand la cause ou l'auteur des faits est évident, inconnu, sans importance ou volontairement passé sous silence.

  Dinner will **be served** shortly. On va bientôt se mettre à table.

  My car **was stolen** last night. On a volé ma voiture hier soir.

  The farm **was sold** to a young couple. La ferme a été vendue à un jeune couple.

  I **was told** he spent several years in prison. On m'a dit qu'il a passé plusieurs années en prison.

• On précisera le complément d'agent quand il apporte une information essentielle au sens de la phrase.

He **was** betray**ed** by his own father! Il a été trahi par son propre père !

Le passif et la traduction de « on »

• Le passif étant plus fréquent en anglais qu'en français, on est souvent confronté à l'impossibilité d'une traduction littérale.

What was to **be done**? Que fallait-il donc faire ?

He **was driven** to his office. On le conduisit au bureau.

• D'autre part, ***one*** n'est pas aussi courant que « **on** » en français. Le passif est plus fréquent (voir également ***we, you, they***, → p. 130).

Paul **is** want**ed** on the phone. **On** demande Paul au téléphone.

We **were** refus**ed** admittance to the pub. **On** nous refusa l'accès au pub.

RÉCAPITULONS

- Le passif se construit avec l'auxiliaire *be* qui doit être conjugué.
- Il est indispensable de connaître le participe passé des verbes irréguliers.
- Le passif est beaucoup plus courant en anglais qu'en français.

SE TESTER QUIZ

1 Choisissez la bonne réponse.

1. He ... English when he was very young.
- [ ] **a.** had taught
- [ ] **b.** was teaching
- [ ] **c.** was taught

2. She ... a new computer next week.
- [ ] **a.** will be given
- [ ] **b.** will have given
- [ ] **c.** will have been given

3. The detective suddenly realized that he ... .
- [ ] **a.** has been followed
- [ ] **b.** was being followed
- [ ] **c.** is followed

4. His mobile phone ..., so he couldn't get in touch with Jane.
- [ ] **a.** is stealing
- [ ] **b.** is stolen
- [ ] **c.** had been stolen

5. The butter must ... in the fridge.
- [ ] **a.** is keeping
- [ ] **b.** is kept
- [ ] **c.** be kept

6. Their house was later reported ... .
- [ ] **a.** being haunted
- [ ] **b.** to be haunted
- [ ] **c.** be haunted

S'ENTRAÎNER

2 Mettez les phrases à la voix passive. Précisez le complément d'agent uniquement si cela est nécessaire.

1. The gang will probably eliminate him.
2. New designers have completely revamped *(rénover)* her apartment.
3. The detective would have uncovered the plot *(complot)* if he hadn't been shot down.
4. Both governments are taking serious precautions.
5. The president will delay payment to foreign companies.
6. They were exploring new planets.
7. A young man gave her a red rose.
8. They lent the President a yacht for his holiday.
9. Several doctors advised her to quit smoking.
10. People believe flying is safer than driving.

3 Il est impossible de faire une traduction littérale des phrases suivantes : proposez une traduction aussi naturelle que possible.

1. Paul was reminded of his promise.
2. I don't like being told what I should do.
3. There was not a sound to be heard.
4. We were kept waiting for over three hours!
5. The private eye *(détective privé)* understood he was given a chance to prove his innocence.
6. Haggis *(la panse de brebis farcie)* is not eaten in Scotland only.
7. John saw Jane to *(accompagner qqn jusqu'à)* the door and was told how nice he was.
8. One can't let an innocent be accused!
9. I realized the house across the street was being pulled down *(démolir)*.
10. Few guests were left in the room.

SE TESTER

1 1. **c.** He **was taught** English when he was very young.
2. **a.** She **will be given** a new computer next week.
3. **b.** The detective suddenly realized that he **was being followed**.
4. **c.** His mobile phone **had been stolen**, so he couldn't get in touch with Jane.
5. **c.** The butter must **be kept** in the fridge.
6. **b.** Their house was later reported **to be haunted**.

S'ENTRAÎNER

2 1. He will probably **be eliminated by the gang**.
2. Her apartment **has been** completely **revamped by new designers**.
3. The plot **would have been uncovered by the detective** if he hadn't been shot down.
4. Serious precautions **are being taken by both governments**.
5. Payment to foreign companies **will be delayed by the president**.
6. New planets **were being explored**.
7. She **was given** a red rose **by a young man**. / A red rose **was given** to her **by a young man**.

8. The president **was lent** a yacht for his holiday. / A yacht **was lent** to the president for his holiday.
9. She **was advised** to quit smoking **by several doctors**.
10. Flying **is believed** to be safer than driving.

3 **1.** On rappela à Paul la promesse qu'il avait faite.
2. Je n'aime pas que l'on me dise ce que je devrais faire.
3. On n'entendait aucun bruit.
4. On nous a fait attendre pendant plus de trois heures !
5. Le détective privé comprit qu'on lui donnait une chance de prouver son innocence.
6. Il n'y a pas qu'en Écosse que l'on mange de la panse de brebis farcie.
7. John accompagna Jane jusqu'à la porte et s'entendit dire combien il était charmant.
8. On ne peut pas laisser accuser un innocent !
9. Je compris qu'on démolissait la maison en face de chez moi.
10. Il restait peu d'invités dans la pièce.

CHAPITRE

21 La modalité

Les modaux sont des outils qui permettent au locuteur de nuancer et / ou de préciser son point de vue : *She **can** be very aggressive*. Ils peuvent aussi lui permettre d'évaluer le degré de probabilité d'une action ou d'un état : *Kevin's late. He **must** be caught in the traffic. He **will** be furious.*

LA CONSTRUCTION DES MODAUX

- Ils ne sont jamais précédés ni suivis de *to* : I can Ø drive.
- Ils ne prennent jamais de *s* à la troisième personne du singulier : He **may** come.
- Ils ont une forme interrogative et une forme négative **sans** *do / does / did* : "**Can** she swim?" "No she **can't**."
- Un modal ne peut jamais en suivre un autre.

I Le point de vue du locuteur sur le sujet

CAN

Capacité	He can do it. Il peut / sait le faire. He can swim. Il sait nager.
Permission / Requête (registre informel)	"Can I leave the table?" "Yes, you can." « Est-ce-que je peux quitter la table ? » « Oui. »
Offre	Can I help you? Je peux t'aider ?
Caractéristique occasionnelle	He can be really mean. Il lui arrive d'être vraiment méchant.

CAN'T

Impossibilité	I can't swim today, it's too cold. Je ne peux pas nager aujourd'hui, il fait trop froid.
Incapacité	I can't speak German. Je ne sais pas parler allemand.
Refus de permission	"Can I leave?" "No, you can't." « Est-ce-que je peux partir ? » « Non. » (Je ne te le permets pas.)
Interdiction à valeur générale	You can't smoke on the premises. Il est interdit de fumer dans les locaux.
Reproche	Can't you work a little harder? Tu ne peux donc pas travailler un peu plus ?

COULD

Capacité au passé	When I was young, I could jog for hours. Quand j'étais jeune, je pouvais courir pendant des heures. He could fly a plane. Il savait piloter un avion.
Capacité hypothétique (conditionnel français)	I could write a book if I wanted to. Je pourrais écrire un livre si je le voulais.
Demande de permission / Requête (polie)	Could you open the door? Pourriez-vous ouvrir la porte ?
Caractéristique occasionnelle au passé	She could be very arrogant. Il lui arrivait d'être très arrogante.
Conseil / Suggestion	You could be nicer to her, don't you think? Tu pourrais quand même être plus gentil avec elle, non ?
Reproche / Regret	You could have asked me! Tu aurais pu me demander !

COULDN'T

Impossibilité / Incapacité (passé)	She couldn't come last year. Elle n'a pas pu venir l'année dernière.
Incapacité hypothétique (conditionnel français)	He couldn't win even if he wanted to. Il ne pourrait pas gagner, même s'il le voulait.
Interdiction / Refus de permission (passé)	Mum told us that we couldn't go to the cinema. Maman nous a dit qu'on n'avait pas le droit d'aller au cinéma
Interdiction générale (passé)	She couldn't smoke in the office. Elle n'était pas autorisée à fumer au bureau.

MAY

Autorisation (souvent officielle)	Photos may be taken in the museum. Les photos sont autorisées dans le musée.
Demande de permission (plus polie que *can*)	May I open the window? Puis-je ouvrir la fenêtre ?
Souhait	May it last! Pourvu que ça dure !

MAY NOT

Interdiction (souvent officielle)	Visitors may not walk on the grass. Les visiteurs ne sont pas autorisés à marcher sur les pelouses.

MIGHT

Conseil / Suggestion (poli)	You might buy a present for her. Peut-être pourriez-vous lui acheter un cadeau ?
Reproche	You might have tried harder. Tu aurais pu essayer avec plus de conviction.
Regret	I might have written sooner. J'aurais pu / dû écrire plus tôt.

MUST

Ordre / Obligation (émanant du locuteur)	I must try harder. Il faut que je fasse des efforts. (C'est ma décision.)
Style indirect (renvoi au passé)	She told me I must go. Elle m'a ordonné de partir.

MUST OU *HAVE TO* ?

- *Must* indique que le locuteur s'impose ou impose l'obligation en question. Avec *have to* l'obligation ou la contrainte est indépendante du bon vouloir du locuteur.

I must pay him back. Je dois le rembourser. (Moi, je me dis que c'est mon devoir de...)
I have to pay this parking fine. Il faut que je paie cette contravention. (Je n'ai pas le choix.)
You must apologize. Tu dois présenter tes excuses. (Moi, qui te parle, je t'ordonne de...)

- On emploie *have to*, et non *must* au *present perfect* et au passé.

He has had to go to London this week. Il a fallu qu'il aille à Londres cette semaine.
He had to pay him back. Il lui a fallu le rembourser.
He had had to help her before. Il avait déjà dû l'aider.

MUSTN'T

Interdiction	She mustn't play with matches. Elle n'a pas le droit de jouer avec des allumettes.

MUSTN'T OU *DON'T HAVE TO / NEEDN'T* ?

Distinguez *mustn't* (interdiction) et *needn't* ou *don't have to* (absence de nécessité, d'obligation).
You are exhausted, you mustn't drive. Tu es épuisé, tu ne dois pas conduire. (Moi, le locuteur, je te l'interdis.)
You don't have to drive. / You needn't drive. Il n'est pas nécessaire que tu prennes la voiture.

WILL

Requête / Proposition polie	"Will you marry me?" « Veux-tu m'épouser ? »
Accord, désir, volonté	"Yes I will." « Oui (je veux t'épouser). »
Caractéristique / Propriété du sujet	Boys will be boys! Les garçons, on ne les changera jamais !

WON'T

Refus	I won't talk to you. Je refuse de te parler.

WOULD

Accord, volonté (passé)	She told me she would do it. Elle m'a dit qu'elle acceptait de le faire.
Action ou état habituel (passé)	As a child, he would scream for hours. Quand il était petit, il hurlait pendant des heures.
Requête / Proposition polie (registre plus soutenu)	Would you have dinner with us? Voudriez-vous dîner avec nous ?

WOULDN'T

Refus (passé)	She wouldn't talk to us. Elle refusait de nous parler. My scooter wouldn't start. Mon scooter refusait de démarrer.

SHALL

Offre / Proposition (avec *I* et *we*)	Shall I drive? Veux-tu que je conduise ? Let's go, shall we? On y va, d'accord ?
Prédiction	This time tomorrow I shall be on holiday. À cette heure-ci demain je serai en vacances.
Volonté, détermination	I shall never give up. Jamais je n'abandonnerai.
Instructions	Teachers shall meet every morning. Les professeurs devront se réunir tous les matins.

SHALL NOT / SHAN'T

Engagement / Interdiction absolue (surtout avec *you*)	You shall not kill. Tu ne tueras point.

SHOULD

Conseil / Suggestion	You should stop smoking. Tu devrais arrêter de fumer.
Reproche	You should have warned me. Tu aurais dû me prévenir.
Regret	I should have known better. J'aurais dû me méfier.

SHOULDN'T

Reproche /Conseil	You shouldn't drive so fast. Tu devrais conduire moins vite. She shouldn't have bought that house. Elle n'aurait pas dû acheter cette maison.

II Les degrés de probabilité

Le locuteur dit qu'un fait est plus ou moins probable, possible, éventuel, certain, etc.

Forte probabilité

MUST (quasi certitude)	She must be exhausted. Elle doit être épuisée. She must have worked late last night. Elle a dû travailler tard hier soir.
CAN'T (quasi certitude que qqch. est impossible, inexact)	What? That can't be true! Comment ? C'est impossible ! He can't have lost the keys! Il est impossible qu'il ait perdu les clés !
WILL	This will be Ted. Ça, c'est sûrement Ted. I will certainly do it tomorrow. Je le ferai certainement demain.

SHOULD	This should work. Ça devrait marcher. He should come / should be coming tomorrow. Il y a de fortes chances qu'il vienne demain.

ATTENTION !
Mustn't n'exprime que l'interdiction. La forte improbabilité est exprimée par *can't*.

Probabilité moyenne ou faible

COULD	It could be a slug. Ça pourrait être une limace. She could have seen the man. Il se pourrait qu'elle ait vu l'homme. / Peut-être a-t-elle vu l'homme. He could come / could be coming tomorrow. Il se pourrait qu'il vienne demain.
MAY	She may have seen Ada. Il se peut qu'elle ait vu Ada. He may come / may be coming tomorrow. Il se peut qu'il vienne demain. / Peut-être viendra t-il demain.
MIGHT (très hypothétique)	She might be Dutch. Il se pourrait qu'elle soit hollandaise. She might have had a nightmare. Il se pourrait qu'elle ait fait un cauchemar. He might come / might be coming tomorrow. Il se pourrait qu'il vienne demain.

ADVERBES ET NOMS
Certains adverbes et noms peuvent aussi exprimer les degrés de probabilité.

adverbs	nouns
possibly, perhaps, maybe	possibility
probably, doubtlessly	probability
certainly, definitely, without doubt, undoubtedly	certainty

III Condition et hypothèse

Le modal se trouve toujours dans la **principale**.

- **Expression de la condition**

  If + présent → ***will*** dans la principale

  If you read carefully, you will understand.
  Si tu lis attentivement, tu comprendras.

- **Expression de l'hypothèse : irréel du présent**

  If + prétérit → ***would*** dans la principale

  If I knew the truth, I would tell you.
  Si je connaissais la vérité, je te le dirais.

- **Expression de l'hypothèse : irréel du passé**

  If + *past perfect* → ***would*** **+** ***have*** **+ participe passé** dans la principale

  You wouldn't have flunked your exams if you had worked!
  Tu n'aurais pas raté tes examens si tu avais travaillé !

  Had I known, I would have come! (construction fréquente avec *know*)
  Si j'avais su, je serais venu.

IV Emplois particuliers de *should*

- Dans les **propositions en *that*** et après des **adjectifs** exprimant une opinion, un jugement, une émotion : *necessary, urgent, important, essential, strange, typical, odd, funny, surprising, embarrassing*, etc.

  It is odd that he **should** ask such a question.
  C'est étrange qu'il pose une telle question.

- Dans les **propositions en *that*** après des **verbes** exprimant un ordre, une exigence : *suggest, insist, demand* (exiger), *order, recommend*, etc.

  Ann insisted that he **should** leave right away.
  Anne insista pour qu'il parte immédiatement.

- Dans des **propositions négatives exprimant le but** *(so that... not)*.

  He invited them so that they **should** not feel excluded.
  Il les invita afin qu'ils ne se sentent pas à l'écart.

RÉCAPITULONS

- Un modal permet d'exprimer le point de vue du locuteur.
- Il n'est jamais suivi d'un autre auxiliaire de modalité.

SE TESTER QUIZ

1 Choisissez la bonne réponse.

1. It ... cold last night: everything is frozen outside.
☐ **a.** must have been ☐ **b.** could be ☐ **c.** might be

2. What's the matter with David? Do you think he ... ill?
☐ **a.** shall be ☐ **b.** might be ☐ **c.** will be

3. How selfish of you! You ... her.
☐ **a.** might have helped ☐ **b.** will help ☐ **c.** can help

4. Had I known he was such a terrible driver, I ... him my car.
☐ **a.** wouldn't have lent ☐ **b.** wouldn't lend ☐ **c.** would lend

5. She ... sell her house unless she is offered a decent price for it.
☐ **a.** would ☐ **b.** may ☐ **c.** won't

6. "... you marry me, Ken?"
"Thanks, but no thanks!"
☐ **a.** Shall ☐ **b.** Can ☐ **c.** Will

S'ENTRAÎNER

2 Traduisez. Utilisez un modal dans les segments soulignés.

1. Tu <u>aurais pu</u> faire attention : tu as failli *(almost)* casser ce verre !
2. Tu <u>sais</u> faire la cuisine ?
3. Cette piscine <u>peut</u> être vidée *(be emptied)* en deux heures.
4. Tu <u>veux</u> du poulet ou du bœuf ? Décide-toi *(make up your mind)* !
5. <u>Et si on</u> achetait des glaces ?
6. Je <u>refuse de</u> te parler parce que tu ne sais pas garder un secret.

3 Complétez ces phrases avec le modal qui convient. Déterminez pour chaque phrase le sens du modal utilisé.

1. Money and valuables *(objets de valeur)* ...... be left in the hotel safe *(coffre-fort)*.
2. ...... you listen to me, please?
3. She was amazing! She ...... play this sonata at the age of four.
4. She just ...... obey, she is impossible!
5. Before he retired *(prendre sa retraite)*, my father ...... leave his office at 9 p.m. every single day!

6. That was a very rude thing to say! You ...... apologize.
7. Come on! There ...... be many people in France who don't know the name of their president! The French aren't that ignorant!
8. I ...... have loved to see her but she was not available *(disponible)*.
9. I ...... paint the kitchen purple but I haven't quite decided yet.
10. You ...... have asked her: it ...... have been nicer.
11. He ...... not be the brightest guy in the world, but I like him.
12. "Laura, ... you marry me?"
"No, I ...."
13. Oh dear! Lily won't play with Sam. He ...... be crying soon!
14. She looked all over the house but ...... find her keys anywhere.
15. It is imperative that he ...... understand that he ...... respect some rules.

4 Traduisez ces phrases en exprimant des degrés de probabilité.

1. Il y a une lettre pour toi ; c'est très certainement ton ex, il t'aime toujours, tu sais.
2. Le Real de Madrid prit un bon départ *(start well)* et aurait pu mener *(take a lead)* si un joueur n'avait pas tapé dans le poteau *(hit the post)*.
3. Il se peut qu'il ne travaille pas très vite, mais au moins il est fiable *(reliable)* !
4. Elle est partie il y a neuf heures : son avion devrait être en train de se poser à San Francisco.
5. Il se pourrait qu'il me téléphone demain.
6. Impossible que j'aie tort : c'est moi le prof, je te rappelle !

SE TESTER

1 **1. a.** It **must have been** cold last night: everything is frozen outside.
2. b. What's the matter with David? Do you think he **might be** ill?
3. a. How selfish of you! You **might have helped** her.
4. a. Had I known he was such a terrible driver, I **wouldn't have lent** him my car.
5. c. She **won't** sell her house unless she is offered a decent price for it.
6. c. "**Will** you marry me, Ken?"
"Thanks, but no thanks!"

S'ENTRAÎNER

2 **1.** You **could / might have** been more careful: you almost broke that glass.
2. **Can** you cook?
3. This swimming pool **can** be emptied in two hours.
4. **Will** you have chicken or beef? Make up your mind!
5. Let's buy ice creams, **shall** we?
6. I **won't** talk to you because you can't keep a secret.

3 **1.** may / can / must / should **(autorisation officielle / possibilité / obligation / conseil)**
2. will / would / could **(volonté / requête / requête)**
3. could **(capacité au passé)**
4. won't / can't **(refus / incapacité)**
5. would **(habitude au passé)**
6. should / might / must **(conseil / suggestion / ordre)**
7. can't (**quasi-certitude** : Il n'y a certainement pas beaucoup de Français qui ne…)
8. would **(conditionnel passé)**
9. may / could / might **(incertitude / degré d'incertitude plus fort)**
10. should … would **(reproche … conditionnel passé)**
11. may (**incertitude** : il se peut que…)
12. will **(volonté)** / won't **(refus)**
13. will **(prédiction)**
14. couldn't **(incapacité au passé)**
15. should … must **(proposition en *that…* / ordre)**

4 **1.** There's a letter for you; this **will** be your ex, he's still in love (with you), you know.
2. Real Madrid started well and **could** have taken a lead if a player hadn't hit the post.
3. He **may** not work very fast but at least he is reliable!
4. She left nine hours ago: her plane **should** be landing in San Francisco.
5. He **might** give me a phone call / **might** call me tomorrow.
6. I **can't** be wrong: let me remind you that I am the teacher!

CHAPITRE

22 Le discours indirect

Le discours indirect sert à rapporter des paroles. Le passage du style direct au style indirect implique un certain nombre d'aménagements grammaticaux et syntaxiques.

I Le fonctionnement

Exemple de discours direct

"Would you like a cup of coffee, Tom?"
"Yes, ma'am, I would," I said nervously.
"Why do you call me ma'am? I believe we're exactly the same age."
"Good home training. And nervousness."
"Why are you nervous? Do you take anything with your coffee?"
"Cream and sugar. [...]"
"Have you ever met a psychiatrist before?" she asked.

Pat Conroy, *The Prince of Tides*, 1986.

Transposition au discours indirect

Observez les changements opérés quand on transpose cet extrait au style indirect.

- Ici, nous adoptons le point de vue de Tom.

She asked me if I would like a cup of coffee. I told her / I replied nervously that I would (like one). She asked me why I called her "ma'am" as she believed we were exactly the same age. I answered that it was good home training and nervousness. She wanted to know why I was nervous and then asked me if I took anything with my coffee. I told her I took (it with) cream and sugar. She eventually asked me if I had ever met a psychiatrist before.

- Si on avait adopté le point de vue du personnage féminin, il aurait fallu commencer ainsi :

I asked him if he would like a cup of coffee. He told me / He replied that...

• Et si on avait choisi un regard extérieur :

She asked Tom if he would like a cup of coffee. He told her...

Le passage au style indirect n'est pas la simple retranscription de ce qui est dit ou a été dit, c'est aussi un **changement de point de vue** qui génère des modifications grammaticales (temps, pronoms...) et syntaxiques (ordre des mots, ponctuation...). Parfois, il nécessite aussi des étoffements : verbes introductifs en début de phrase.

"Cream and sugar." → I told her I took (it with) cream and sugar.

II Les modifications grammaticales

A Pronoms, possessifs

"I like her," I said. → I said (that) I liked her.

"I am lost," **she** said. → **She** said (that) **she** was lost.

"**We** are late," **they** admitted. → **They** admitted (that) **they** were late.

"**You**'re a fool," she said to me. → She said (to me) (that) I was a fool.

"**You** are an idiot!" Bill said to Ken. → Bill said to Ken (that) **he** was an idiot.

"**You** are all fools," he said to **them**. → He said (to them) (that) **they** were all fools.

"I'll write **you** a letter," she said to us. → She promised (that) she would write **us** a letter.

"Give **me your** book," she said. → She asked me to give **her my** book.

"Clyde is **our** only child." → They told me (that) Clyde was **their** only child.

"The book on the shelf is **mine**," she said. → She said (that) the book on the shelf was **hers**.

B Temps dans les subordonnées

Présent → présent

"I'm not feeling very well, tell the teacher, please." → "Miss! Harry says he **isn't** feeling very well."

Présent → prétérit

"I want a glass of wine." → She said she wanted a glass of wine.

"I am not working." → He said that he was not working.

- *Present perfect* → *past perfect*

  "I have not finished." → He added that he had not finished.

  "I have been gardening." → He explained that he had been gardening.

- Prétérit → *past perfect*

  "I woke up early." → He told us that he had woken up early.

  "I was travelling." → He told them he had been travelling.

- *Past perfect* → *past perfect*

  "I had never been so happy." → He said he had never been so happy.

ATTENTION

Ces changements ne sont pas systématiques.

"New York **is** the most exciting city," Paul said. → Paul said New York **is** the most exciting city. (C'est toujours le cas au moment où je parle.)

"When I live**d** in San Diego, I often travelled to Mexico." → He mentioned that when he lived in San Diego, he often travelle**d** to Mexico. (passé)

C Modaux

Will → would : "I'**ll** talk to you later." → She said she **would** talk to me later.

Can → could : "**Can** I leave?" → He asked me if he **could** leave.

May → might : "She **may** be sick." → He informed us that she **might** be sick.

Must → must : "You **must** be more careful." → She told me I **must** be more careful.

Have to → had to : "I **have to** talk to her." → He confessed that he **had to** talk to her.

(contrainte extérieure, voir *must* et *had to*, → p. 207.)

D Repères spatiaux / temporels

here → there

now → then

today → that day

yesterday → the day before, the previous day

tomorrow → the following day, the next day, the day after

the day after tomorrow → two days later

next Tuesday → the following Tuesday

next week / month / year → the following week, the next month, the year after

six months ago → six months before

last Friday → the previous Friday

last week / month / year → the previous week / month / year

this / these → that / those (→ p. 117 à 119)

ATTENTION

- Les changements de repères ne sont pas systématiques.

Ben said he will / would meet me **here.** (Pas de changement de lieu → **here.**)
I saw Lisa last week and she said: "I want to go to New York **next year**." → I saw Lisa last week and she told me she wants / want**ed** to go to New York **next year.**
(Les paroles de Lisa sont rapportées durant l'année où elle les a prononcées → **next year** et non pas **the following year**).

- Il y a passage de **this** vers **that** (singulier) et de **these** vers **those** (pluriel) si les propos rapportés se situent dans un passé suffisamment lointain.

"I am leaving **this** week." → He told me he was leaving **this** week. (cette semaine)
→ He told me he was leaving **that** week. Il m'a dit qu'il partait cette semaine-**là**.
(semaine révolue au moment où l'on parle)

III Étoffements et changements syntaxiques

A Verbes introductifs

- Exemples : *say, acknowledge* (admettre), *add* (ajouter), *admit, answer, declare, expect, explain, insist, mention, promise, reply, report, state* (déclarer), *suggest, tell*...

- ***Say* ou *tell*** ? Ils ont souvent le même sens mais ne se construisent pas de la même manière.

• *Say* se construit avec une subordonnée éventuellement introduite par <u>*that*</u> ou bien avec un <u>complément d'objet direct</u> suivi obligatoirement de <u>*to*</u>.

She said (<u>that</u>) she would come.

Ann said <u>goodbye</u> <u>to</u> me and left.

What did you say <u>to</u> the police?

• *Tell* est toujours suivi d'un <u>complément</u> (nom ou pronom).

Kathy told <u>me</u> / <u>Richard</u> / <u>the police</u> (that) she knew the truth.

B Les structures affirmatives et négatives

Aucun changement syntaxique.

"I've never met the Wilsons."
→ He explained that he had never met the Wilsons.

C Les structures interrogatives

Les verbes introductifs les plus fréquents sont *ask, enquire about* (se renseigner sur), *want to know, wonder...*

- Questions fermées *(Yes / No)*

"Do you like him?" she asked.
→ She wanted to know **if / whether** I liked him.

- Questions ouvertes

"When are you leaving?" he asked.
→ He asked me when I was leaving.

ATTENTION !
Notez l'ordre des mots : Nobody knows where Pertenhall is.

D Verbes suivis de l'infinitif complet (ordre, intention, promesse...)

Les verbes introductifs les plus fréquents sont *advise* (conseiller), *agree, ask, beg* (prier de), *demand* (exiger), *encourage, forbid* (interdire), *offer, order, tell somebody to, threaten* (menacer), *urge* (inciter à), *want, warn* (avertir)...

"You should go, Frank."
→ He told / asked / ordered Frank **to** go.

"Don't shout," she told them.
→ She told / asked / ordered them **not to** shout.

"It's OK, I'll do it for you," she said.
→ She **agreed to** do it for me / us.

"The theatre could be built next to the shopping centre," they said.
→ They **proposed** to build the theatre next to the shopping centre.

ATTENTION

- Certains verbes admettent deux structures.

They promised me **to** do it. / They promised **to** do it for me.

- Cas particulier : *suggest*

"Why don't we walk the dog?" he said.

He suggested (that) they (should) walk / (that) they walked the dog.

He suggested walking the dog.

(*Suggest* + *-ing* signifie que le sujet de *suggest* est lui aussi concerné.)

"Why don't you have a hot bath?" she said.

She suggested (that) he should / might have / (that) he had a hot bath.

She suggested (that) he ha**ve** a hot bath.

(Ici, *have* est un subjonctif.)

E Étoffements et explicitations

Une transposition au discours indirect nécessite parfois une explicitation (verbe, auxiliaire de modalité, expression).

"I'm sorry I behaved so badly." → He apologized for behaving so badly.

"Have a merry Christmas!" → He wished me a merry Christmas.

"And remember that it may snow," the guide said. → The guide reminded us that it might snow.

RÉCAPITULONS

- Faites bien attention à la concordance des temps lorsque vous passez du style direct au style indirect.
- N'oubliez pas les autres aménagements syntaxiques éventuellement nécessaires, notamment en ce qui concerne les pronoms.

SE TESTER QUIZ

1 Choisissez la bonne transposition au discours indirect.

1. "Brad doesn't like me," she said to me in a low voice.
- ☐ **a.** She said to me in a low voice that Brad doesn't like me.
- ☐ **b.** She said to me in a low voice that Brad didn't like me.
- ☐ **c.** She said to me in a low voice that Brad didn't like her.

2. "When is the next train?" he asked.
- ☐ **a.** He asked when the next train was.
- ☐ **b.** He asked when the next train is.
- ☐ **c.** He asked when is the next train.

3. "Stop complaining," the manager said to his exhausted secretary.
- ☐ **a.** The manager told his exhausted secretary to stop complaining.
- ☐ **b.** The manager told his exhausted secretary stop complaining.
- ☐ **c.** The manager told his exhausted secretary she stopped complaining.

4. "Don't kiss me again!" he implored her.
- ☐ **a.** He implored her that she didn't kiss him again.
- ☐ **b.** He implored her that she won't kiss him again.
- ☐ **c.** He implored her not to kiss him again.

5. Two minutes ago she said to us: "I'll give you the results tomorrow."
- ☐ **a.** Two minutes ago she said to us that she would give us the results tomorrow.
- ☐ **b.** Two minutes ago she said to us that she would give us the results the following day.
- ☐ **c.** Two minutes ago she said to us that she would give us the results the next day.

6. Three months ago, they said to us: "We'll call you next week."
- ☐ **a.** Three months ago, they said to us they will call us next week.
- ☐ **b.** Three months ago, they said to us they would call us next week.
- ☐ **c.** Three months ago, they said to us they would call us the following week.

S'ENTRAÎNER

2 Mettez les phrases suivantes au style indirect.

1. "I'm not going back to school," she announced.
2. "I didn't mean to upset you," he insisted.

3. "I won't be late again," the teacher promised.
4. "I can't understand what you wrote," she complained.
5. "You should give him a call tomorrow," he added.
6. "Have I done the right thing?" he wondered.
7. "Can we stop at the next village?" she asked me.
8. "Where did you put the keys?" she wanted to know.
9. "How do you spell *charisma*?" she asked me.
10. "Why don't we stop for a drink?" she suggested.

3 Mettez ces phrases au style indirect en utilisant les amorces proposées.

1. "If I leave early, I'll avoid heavy traffic." → *He expected...*
2. "I will fight global warming." → *The president promised...*
3. "Don't worry about the price." → *She told...*
4. "You shouldn't underestimate him, believe me!" → *She urged...*
5. "Stop arguing, please!" → *She begged...*

4 Mettez l'extrait suivant au style indirect. Introduisez les étoffements que vous jugerez utiles. Gardez le point de vue de la jeune femme (*I* dans le texte, *she* étant sa mère).

Une mère et sa fille ont été menacées par un ancien espion.

"I made a mistake," she said, suddenly, making me start.
"What?"
"He knows you're my daughter. He knows your name."
"So what?" I said. "He also knows you've got him cold. Everything's going to come out. He can't lay a finger on you. You told him – you challenged him to pick up the phone."
She thought about it.
"Maybe you're right... Maybe that's enough. Maybe he won't make any calls. But he might leave something written. [...] It would be safer to leave something written, you see, because..." [...]
"Because what?"
"Because he'll be dead by tomorrow morning."
"Dead? How can he be dead tomorrow morning?"

William Boyd, *Restless*, 2006.

make sb start: faire sursauter qqn
lay a finger on sb: atteindre qqn
get sb cold: coincer qqn
challenge sb to: défier qqn de

SE TESTER

1 1. c. – 2. a. – 3. a. – 4. c. – 5. a. – 6. c.

S'ENTRAÎNER

2 1. She announced that she was not going back to school.
2. He insisted that he hadn't meant to upset me / us / him / her / them.
3. The teacher promised that he / she wouldn't be late again / promised not to be late again.
4. She complained that she couldn't understand what I / he / she / we / they had written.
5. He added that I / she / he / we / they should give him a call the next day / tomorrow. *(Si les propos sont rapportés le jour où ils ont été prononcés.)*
6. He wondered if he had done the right thing.
7. She asked me if we could stop at the next village.
8. She wanted to know where I / she / he / we / they had put the keys.
9. She asked me how I spelt *charisma*.
10. She suggested that we / they (should) stop / She suggested that we / they stopped / She suggested stopping for a drink.

3 1. He expected to avoid heavy traffic if he left early.
2. The president promised to fight / that he would fight global warming.
3. She told me / us / him / her / them not to worry about the price.
4. She urged me / us / him / her / them not to underestimate him.
5. She begged me / us / him / her / them to stop arguing.

4 Suddenly she said she had made a mistake and it made me start. I asked her what she had just said. She answered that he / the man knew that I was her daughter and that he knew my name. I replied that it didn't matter. I told her that he also knew she had got him cold. I added that everything was going to come out and that he couldn't lay a finger on her. I also reminded her that she had told him, even challenged him to pick up the phone. She thought about it. She finally admitted that maybe I was right. That maybe that was enough and that he wouldn't make any calls. She added that he might leave something written though. [...] She explained to me it would be safer for him to leave something written. I asked her why. She answered that he would be dead by the following morning. I couldn't believe my ears. I asked her how he could possibly be dead the following morning.

Crédits textes

Achevé d'imprimer en Espagne par Grafo
Dépôt légal n° 99467-8/02 - septembre 2017